Catch your limit—
Limit your catch.

SECRET RECIPES

RECIPES

FROM A CANADIAN FISHING GUIDE

DARRYL CHORONZEY

Author's note:
Fish illustrations courtesy of Govt. of Canada, Fisheries & Oceans
Illustrations used in the chapters on filleting and knife care
are used with permission of Normark
Other drawings by Marsha Batchelor
Illustrations & text in the chapters on Home Pickling and
Nutritional Values of Fish are reproduced with permission of
the University of Wisconsin Sea Grant Institute

Published by

**krause
publications**

700 E. State Street • Iola, WI 54990-0001
Telephone: 715/445-2214

Please call or write for our free catalog of outdoor publications.
Our toll-free number to place an order or obtain a free catalog is 800-258-0929 or
please use our regular business telephone 715-445-2214 for editorial comment
and further information.

Library of Congress Catalog Number: 98-87359
ISBN: 0-87341-726-7

Printed in the United States of America

DEDICATION

This book is dedicated to all those who strive to keep our lakes and rivers pure and, in doing so, ensure better fishing for tomorrow's children.

Photo above: The author's wife, Monica Choronzey, who helped compile and test the recipes found in this book.

ABOUT THE
AUTHOR

Darryl Choronzey is the editor/publisher of the *Ontario Fisherman* Magazine, Ontario's only all-fishing publication. Living near Wiarton, Ontario, the author has the opportunity to fish many of the province's best lakes and rivers. *In the photo above, the author poses with a 68 lb. Chinook Salmon caught at Kenia River, Alaska.*

CONTENTS

ANATOMY OF A FISH

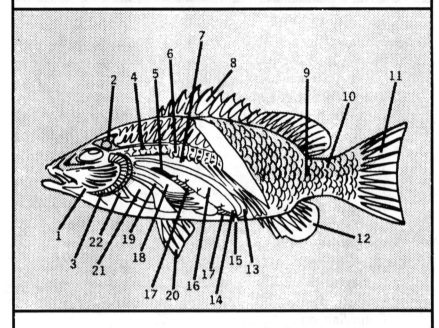

1. Gill Rakers	12. Anal Fin
2. Brain	13. Urinary Bladder
3. Gills	14. Ovary
4. Spinal Cord	15. Vent
5. Spleen	16. Fatty Tissue
6. Kidney	17. Intestine
7. Gas Bladder	18. Stomach
8. Dorsal Fin	19. Gall Bladder
9. Lateral Line	20. Pelvic Fin
10. Caudal Peduncle	21. Liver
11. Caudal Fin	22. Heart

INTRODUCTION

North America is blessed with thousands of miles of prime fishing water. Without a doubt our continent boasts the best and most diversified sport fishery on the globe.

It is left to us to enjoy this sport fishery, the challenge of the battle between fish and man, and also the end result whereby we have the opportunity to relish the tastiest of meals imaginable. But it is also left to us to protect this sport fishery. To accomplish this, we must protect our fish stocks. No matter how large North America might be, we must respect even the tiniest stream or the smallest pond. We have already lost much of our environment to neglect, let's lose no more.

The recipes found within cover many of the sport fish found in North America. My advice to the reader is to sample these recipes, then experiment. Many of these recipes can also be used with other fish species.

Enjoy the outdoors, enjoy its fish and enjoy the pleasure they will both provide for you.

May your hooks always be sharp, your knots strong, and your lines tight.

Darryl Choronzey

Producer / Host
Going Fishing

STORING IS IMPORTANT!

Game fish is at its best fresh. Fresh fish should be used as soon as possible. If refrigerated, wash fish, remove moisture, and wrap it in waxed paper.

A constant temperature of below -10°F is recommended for all frozen fish. Packages of fish should be kept unopened while in the freezer to prevent frost burn. Fish should only be kept for short periods in the freezer. Fatty fish—2 months. Lean fish—3 months.

If a fish must be thawed before cooking (frying, stuffing) it should be done at refrigerator temperature. Thawed fish should be cooked as soon as possible. Never refreeze fish.

THINGS TO REMEMBER

1) Do not overcook fish. Cooked fish should be moist.
2) Cooking is complete when the flesh flakes readily.
3) Other than panfrying or stuffing, do not thaw fish before cooking.
4) Serve fish immediately after cooking while it is still hot, tender and juicy.

THE WAYS TO COOK FISH

BROILING

Fish steaks are only usually turned once while broiling. A moderately hot (375°-400°F) broiler is best. Strips of bacon can be applied to the fish or butter or margarine can be brushed on. After the fish is turned apply salt and pepper to the cooked side. Fillets or steaks require 5 to 8 minutes cooking on each side, whole fish require 10 to 11 minutes on each side, and split fish 6 to 8 minutes. Fish should be positioned 2 to 6 inches from heat source.

BAKING

The tastiest and one of the most common methods of cooking fish is baking. Fish can be baked with or without stuffing. The inside of the fish should be thoroughly dried and then dusted lightly with salt and pepper. Butter, oil or margarine should be rubbed over the outside of the fish or bacon strips placed over the fish. The actual cooking takes place in a greased, uncovered pan. A moderately hot oven (400°F) at the rate of 10 minutes per pound for unstuffed fish and 15 to 20 minutes per pound for stuffed fish.

DEEP FRYING

Fish fillets are dried, dipped into batter and then slowly lowered into hot (375°F) oil. Oil depth should be at least 3 inches to prevent fish from sticking. Depending on thickness of fillet, 4 to 5 minutes of frying should be sufficient.

PAN FRYING

When cooked at 350°F under constantly controlled conditions, pan-dressed fish, fillets and steaks are succulent. Fish are most often dipped in a liquid and then rolled in bread crumbs. With the aid of approximately 1/8 inch of hot oil and a heavy fry pan, the fish is lightly browned on both sides. Cooking time is usually 3 to 4 minutes for each side of the fish. Drain off oil and serve with lemon.

BOILING

Steaks or fillets of soft (salmon, trout, steelhead) finned fish are placed in a basket and lowered into boiling salt water for 12 minutes. If the 8 quart boiling kettle is used, one cup of salt is added to the water. If the 12 quart kettle is used, two cups of salt are added. Fish is drained and served with boiled potatoes, onions and drawn butter.

BARBEQUING

A West Coast method of cooking trout and salmon, the charcoal heat technique prepares fish by means of dry heat. Fillets and steaks are the best suited for the barbecue. Fish should be thawed in advance. Wire grills are recommended because of the tendency of fish to flake easily as it nears completion. Because of the hot dry heat of the charcoal, thicker slices of steak are best and they should also be coated with a barbecue sauce to ensure that the juices are locked in the fish. Fish usually takes from 5 to 10 minutes on each side. Fish should be 4 or 5 inches from coals when cooking.

SMOKING

Salting, drying and heat treatment by smoke are all a part of smoking fish. In most cases a brine is used, with the amount of salt in the brine determining the amount of cure. Brine not only adds flavour to the fish it also firms the flesh. The heat range for Hot Smoking is 120° to 180°F. Alder, apple, hickory and cherry wood are the most common woods used in smoking.

Homemade smokers are constructed from 50-gallon barrels, garbage cans and old refrigerators. The most popular commercial unit is the Little Chief Smoker manufactured by Luhr Jensen and Sons of Hood River, Oregon. See the chapter on smoking fish.

CANNING

A popular West Coast method of preparing and preserving salmon and steelhead is canning. While the canning technique is tasty and also worth the time spent in the preparation, it can also be hazardous. The canning instructions must be followed exactly as the pressure cooker manufacturer stipulates. In most cases, 1/2 pint jars of salmon and pint jars of salmon are pressure cooked at 10 pounds for 90 minutes. Catsup and a small amount of table salt are added to the jars before cooking. Once again, manufacturer's instructions should be followed throughout the process. Again, see the chapter on canning.

POACHING

All poaching consists of is the wrapping of inch thick steaks or fillets of fish in cheesecloth or muslin (a dish towel is often substituted), placed in a wire basket, and then simmered in hot water. One tablespoon of vinegar and 1/2 teaspoon of salt is mixed with each four cups of water. The fish is allowed to simmer for approximately 15 minutes for each pound of fish. The fish is then drained and served with a white sauce. Boullion can be substituted for the water, vinegar and salt mix.

STEAMING

This is much like poaching, except that the wrapped fish is placed on a rack above boiling water. The steaming pot or dish is covered tightly with a lid and the fish is allowed to cook for approximately 15 minutes per pound. The fish is seasoned with salt, pepper and lemon, after it is removed from the steamer.

HOW MUCH IS ENOUGH?

CUT	EXPLANATION	SERVINGS
Whole or round	just as taken from the water	allow 1 pound for one serving.
Dressed or drawn	viscera removed	allowed 1 pound for one serving.
Pan dressed	scaled, eviscerated, with head, tail and fins removed	allow 1 pound for 2 servings.
Steaks	cross section sliced	allow 1 pound for 2 to 3 servings.
Fillets	meaty sides free of bones	allow 1 pound for 3 servings.

FILLETING

The following chapter is reproduced with the kind permission of Normark Inc., Oshawa, Ontario. The chapter is reproduced from *'The Rapala Fishing Guide'* and *'How to Clean a Mess of Fish Without Making a Mess of the Fish.'* These two publications are a must item for every tackle box or home fishing library.

For Walleye, Trout and Fish with Similar Bone Structure

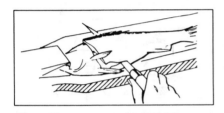

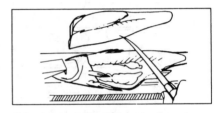

1. Make first cut just behind the gills. Slice down to the bone, then, without removing blade, turn it and slice straight along backbone...

2. ...to the tail. Note that the fillet has been cut away from the rest of the fish. After slicing fillet off at tail, turn fish over and repeat procedure on the other side.

3. With both sides removed, you have cut away both fillets without disturbing fish's entrails. This is the neatest and fastest way to prepare fish.

4. Next step is to remove the rib section. Again, a sharp, flexible knife is important to avoid wasting meat. Insert blade close to rib bones and slice entire section away. This should be done before skin is removed to keep waste to a minimum.

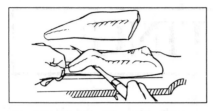

5. Removing the skin from each fillet is simply a matter of inserting the knife at the tail and "cutting" the meat from the skin. Start cut 1/2 inch from tail end of skin, allowing wedge for best grip. With the proper knife, like the "Fish 'N Fillet", it's easily done.

6. Here is each fillet, ready for the pan, or freezer. Note there is no waste. Remember not to overwash fillets. This will preserve tasty juices and keep meat in its firm natural state.

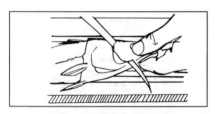

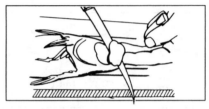

7. Cutting out the "cheeks" is the next important step. Few fishermen know that cheeks are the filet mignon of the fish. Though small, they're tasty and well worth saving.

8. Slice into cheek where indicated then "scoop out" meat with blade, peeling away skin. Repeat on the other side. Many fishermen save cheeks until they have accumulated enough for a real gourmet's delight.

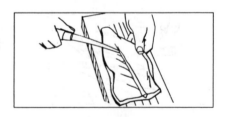

9. Here are all parts of the fish after you've finished. Note fish head, entrails, spine, tail and fins stay intact. This is the neatest way to prepare most game fish and, once you've mastered these few steps, the easiest.

10. Very large walleyes, like northern pike, contain troublesome Y bones. To remove with skin still on, run finger along lateral line of flesh side of fillet, feeling for tiny bones. When located, make wedge-shaped cut, as indicated, and lift out– Y bones will be inside. Then remove skin from other side of fillet (#5 above).

For Northern Pike

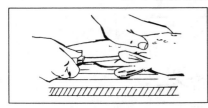

1. Remove two anal fins (ones ahead of tail) by running knife along each side of outside of fin base and attached heavy cartilage, pulling entire assembly free.

2. Fillet fish, with skin still attached, as for walleyes (#1 to #4). With fillet flesh-side up, make cut on angle along the pronounced lateral line. This is first step of removing tiny and troublesome Y bones.

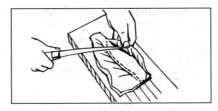

3. Fold over the flap resulting from this incision and cut off all of flesh containing Y bones. Now remove skin from "deboned" fillet as for the walleye (#5).

For Fish with Heavy Rib Structure:
Large Bass, Pike or Salt Water Species

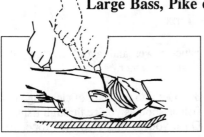

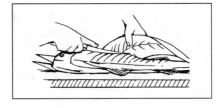

1. Holding head of fish firmly, make first cut at angle indicated, down to but not severing the backbone. Run knife at angle along backbone without cutting through rib cage, to point just behind vent, at which push blade all the way through and, with blade flat against backbone, run knife all the way to tail.

2. Holding free flap of meat aloft, carefully separate fillet from rib cage. Penetrate thin stomach skin to free fillet, turn fish over and repeat process. Now remove skin from outside fillets as for the walleye (#5).

For Panfish Too Small to Fillet

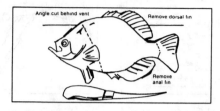

Remove dorsal and anal fins by running knife point along each side of base and pulling free. This will remove many tiny bones from flesh. Scale fish, then behead, by cutting body at an angle behind the gills. This will eliminate most of the rib cage and viscera. Finally, cut off the tail with two slanting incisions that will remove many fine bones.

Steaking Large Fish

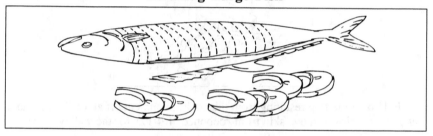

Cut steak 3/4 to 1 1/2 inches thick at right angles to back bone of fish.

Advance Tips

1. Fish are like any other kind of food. Care must be given to preserve the flavour and keep them from spoiling. Most fish species should be cleaned and chilled as quickly as possible.

2. The juices in the flesh of a fish are much like that of good meat. They should be preserved to maintain peak flavour. If you wash your fillets, make certain the water is cold. Never overwash fillets. Avoid flooding meat with a hard-running hose. Many veteran fishermen dry the fillets with a cloth or paper towel and avoid washing the flesh altogether.

3. Get into the habit of cleaning your fish as soon as you're through fishing. Once you've mastered the proper filleting techniques, this takes only a few minutes. You conserve fish and make the trip more fun too.

4. Carry plastic bags for your fillets. One or two will neatly hold a day's catch. The plastic bags chill easily and hold in natural flavour and juices.

Skinning Techniques with a Skinning Board

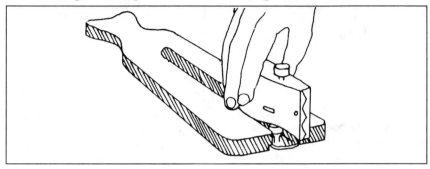

Loosen knurled nut and slide into channel, keeping cone shaped piece on top side of groove. Use knurled nut to loosen and tighten for proper length of fish.

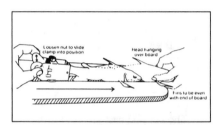

1. Place skin-type fish (catfish or bullhead) on board placing tail in clamp. Adjust for length of fish by loosening knurled nut on top of clamp and slide in slot until head of fish hangs over the end of the board and front fins (pectoral) are even with end of board. Then tighten knurled nut.

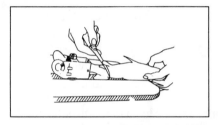

2. Start cut just behind rear dorsal fin at clamp and continue a shallow cut along the top of the fish to the back of the head.

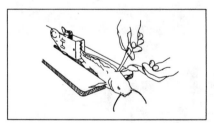

3. Turn the blade and cut downwards to the backbone being careful not to cut through it.

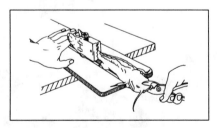

4. Place the board over the end of table. Use a pliers and grip the outside of the head. With the other hand, hold the board firmly.

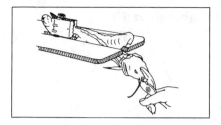

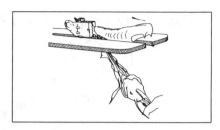

5. Pull down on pliers, forcing the head below the board; and, as you pull, gently twist the head from side to side if necessary to keep skin separating evenly.

6. The head and skin will start to separate from the body taking with it the entrails and inedible parts of the fish. After skin is removed, fish is taken from clamp and tail is cut off.

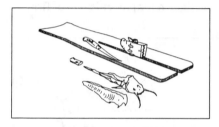

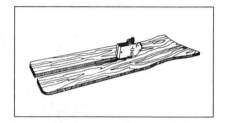

7. Here are all the parts of the fish. The only thing left is to wash the body section lightly in cold water and prepare it with your favourite recipe.

The skin on catfish and bullheads will vary in thickness. This could cause the skin to tear prematurely. If this happens, it can be removed with pliers.

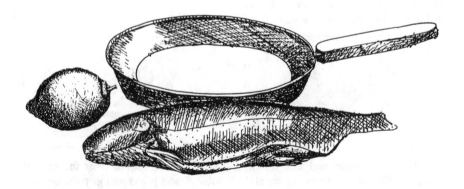

KNIFE SHARPENING

Whether you use a wet or dry stone is not as important as some say. You can get a good edge either way. Both water and oil help float away the metal particles and help bring up a finer edge than the dry method. Most sharpening experts say oil slows down the grinding process slightly, but insures a longer life for the stone.

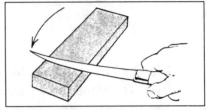

1. To sharpen knife like the Rapala Fish 'N Fillet, lay the blade edge on the stone at a 15° angle. Give each side of the knife about 10 strokes on the fine side of the stone. (If the knife is very dull, give each side of the blade five or six strokes on the coarse side of the stone first.)

2. Work the blade across the stone against the edge (as if cutting toward the stone). Don't press too hard or too light. A steady pressure with steady strokes will do it. Also be careful not to hold the knife too flat on the stone. This will result in a "feather edge" which wears down quickly.

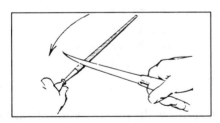

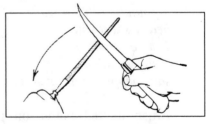

3. Setting the edge of your newly sharpened knife is very important. This is done with steel or strop bought right along with your sharpening stone. The steel does not sharpen your knife, but it realigns the microscopic teeth forming the cutting edge and revives its sharpness.

4. Using only light pressure, draw the blade toward you against the edge (as if slicing into the steel) from heel of knife to point. Knife's edge should be at about 20° (slightly greater angle for hunting knife). About ten strokes on each side of the knife is enough.

WALLEYE

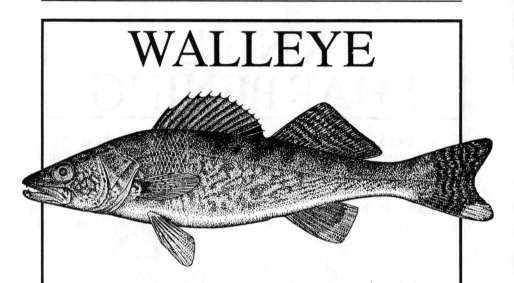

Old Opal Eyes is in a class by himself when it comes to taste. The white flesh and excellent flavour make this species a favorite with anglers throughout Canada, the American Midwest and recently as far west as the Columbia River which divides the states of Oregon and Washington.

WAWA WALLEYE FOIL BAKE

3 pounds of fresh walleye fillets　　*lemon slices*
heavy sheet foil　　*melted butter*
1 sliced tomato　　*1 inch butter squares*
1 sliced onion　　*1 bottle of ale*
salt, pepper and garlic to taste

Brush melted butter on pan. Lay walleye fillets on foil. Sprinkle 1/4 bottle of ale over fish. Lay tomato, onion, butter and lemon slices over fish. Close foil over fish and seal. Bake for 20 minutes at 300°F.

BAKED MOON RIVER WALLEYE

*1 walleye (preferably 5 to 10 pounds) cleaned with head
and fins removed
stuffing:
1 can of oysters   salt, pepper and sage
30 to 40 soda crackers   1/2 pound of bacon
1/2 cup of milk*

Stuffing is prepared by mixing oysters, milk and crackers together. Then add seasoning to taste. The belly cavity of the
walleye is stuffed with dressing and then the flaps are sewn
together. Place fish on rack in roasting dish. Arrange several
strips of bacon on top of fish and also wedge bacon into
grooves where fins were removed. Bake 2 1/2 hours at 250°F
or until walleye is white and flaky.

ST. CLAIR PICKEREL IN BEER BATTER

*4 pounds of fresh walleye fillets   1 teaspoon salt
1 1/2 cups all purpose flour   1 1/2 cups beer
2 eggs   cooking oil*

Place flour in deep bowl. Beat eggs until frothy. Add salt and
beer to eggs. Combine liquids with the flour. Beat until free of
lumps. Coat each fish fillet separately when ready to fry. Deep
fry until light brown in heated oil at 375°F. Serve hot with
lemon and hot rolls.

FISH CAMP WALLEYE FRY

2 to 4 pounds of fresh walleye fillets
1/2 cup milk   *oil or butter*
1 egg   *salt, pepper, onion seasoning*
corn flakes or breadcrumbs

Beat milk and eggs with a fork. Dip fillets (small pieces) in mixture, then in crumbs, making certain fish is completely coated. Slowly submerge fillets into 1/4 inch deep hot oil. Brown both sides. Test with fork for tender white flesh. Serve with catsup, lemon and tartar sauce.

Walleye fillets are unbeatable for a morning's camp fry.

WALLEYE & MUSHROOMS HONEY HARBOUR STYLE

4 large walleye fillets   *1/2 cup white wine*
1 can cream of mushroom soup   *2 tablespoons butter*
1/4 teaspoon salt   *1 tablespoon parsley flakes*
1/4 teaspoon pepper   *1/2 cup milk*
1/4 teaspoon garlic salt   *1 can mushroom pieces*

Arrange walleye fillets in large baking dish. Combine cream of mushroom soup, wine, milk, mushroom pieces and seasonings. Pour over fish. Dab with butter and sprinkle with parsley flakes. Place in oven and bake at approximately 350°F for 25 to 35 minutes.

FRENCH RIVER WALLEYE BROIL

3 pounds of walleye fillets
1 package Shake'n Bake or cracker crumbs
salt, pepper and other seasonings
1/4 cup melted margarine or oil

Rinse fillets in water, shaking off excess water. Place fillets in a bag with Shake 'n Bake or cracker crumbs and cover. Place fillets on broiler pan, brush lightly with melted butter, season to taste and add a small amount of lemon juice. Place under medium heat. As fillets are browning, brush occasionally with butter. Large fillets should be turned once. Serve with lemon wedges, catsup and tartar sauce.

POACHED QUINTE BAY WALLEYE

2 pounds walleye fillets
2 cups milk
1 teaspoon salt
4 tablespoons flour

4 tablespoons melted butter
2 teaspoons lemon juice
1/2 cup sliced stuffed olives

Slice the fillets into serving portions. Simmer slowly in salted milk for 5 to 10 minutes or until fish flakes easily when tested with a fork. Remove from heat. Place fillets on heated platter, keeping hot. Combine flour and melted butter. Add milk slowly. Cook and stir until thickened. Add olives and lemon juice. Pour over fish.

Will serve 6 to 8 anglers.

GRAND RIVER FISH CAKES

1 cup flaked cooked walleye
1 teaspoon minced onion
1/4 teaspoon salt
1 teaspoon lemon juice

1 cup mashed potatoes
2 tablespoons flour
1 egg slightly beaten
cooking oil

Combine fish, onion, seasoning, lemon juice, potatoes and eggs. Make into round cakes. Fry in hot oil. Will serve 4 hungry anglers.

BAKED LEAMINGTON WALLEYE SUPREME

2 pounds walleye fillets
2 cups chopped onion
2 cans undiluted consommé
1 cup catsup

1 1/2 cups sliced dill pickle
4 tablespoons butter
2 tablespoons flour

Saute onions in butter while oven is being preheated to 400°F. Slowly stir in flour and gradually add catsup and consommé. Simmer for 30 minutes, stirring occasionally. Add pickles. Lay walleye in a shallow baking dish and cover with sauce. Bake walleye in oven for 35 minutes or until walleye flakes easily with fork.

PORT BURWELL PICKEREL BAKE

4 medium walleye fillets   1/2 cup fine chopped onion
3 tablespoons fresh chopped dill 1/4 cup water
2/3 cup fine chopped parsley

Cover bottom of baking pan with chopped parsley. Place fish over the parsley. Place onions over fish. Sprinkle remaining ingredients and water over fish and bake in a 350°F preheated oven for 25 minutes.

NAKINA WALLEYE FISH OMELET

1 1/2 cups of cooked flaked walleye
8 to 10 eggs   2 tablespoons cooking oil
salt and pepper to taste   garlic to taste
2 teaspoons bacon grease   1/6 teaspoon dried basil
3 teaspoons chopped onion   5 tablespoons beer
3 tablespoons butter

Heat bacon grease in frying pan. Lightly saute chopped onions. Remove pan from heat and stir fish into onions. In a second large frying pan heat butter. Beat eggs lightly in a bowl and at the same time stir in pepper, salt, basil, garlic, beer and fish mixture from first frying pan. Pour omelet mixture into second frying pan. With heat at medium, lift edges of omelet occasionally so that uncooked portions of egg will run off and cook. Eggs are cooked when the bottom of the omelet is a light gold. The top of the omelet should be soft, but not runny. If eggs should start to stiffen during cooking period lower heat.

This is a meal for the gang at the fishing camp. Six to 10 hungry anglers can devour this breakfast before heading out on the lake.

POINTE AU BARIL SOUR CREAM DELIGHT

2 one pound walleye fillets
1 cup dry white wine
2 cups of sour cream
5 tablespoons chopped onions
salt, pepper & garlic to taste

1 1/2 teaspoons of parsley
small jar chopped pimento
2 tablespoons flour

Preheat oven to 350°F. Set fillets in a lightly greased baking dish or pan. Everything but the pimento are mixed and then spread over fillets. Bake for 25 minutes. Top fillets with pimento and bake for an additional 5 minutes.

MITCHELL'S BAY PICKEREL IN LEMON BATTER

3/4 pound of walleye fillets
1 cup of flour
1 lightly beaten egg
5/8 cup of water

white pepper to taste
salt to taste
2 tablespoons lemon juice
1 teaspoon baking powder

Dry freshly filleted pickerel fillets. Rub salt and pepper into fillets. Mix baking powder into flour. Thoroughly stir together water, lemon juice, egg. Slowly add flour. Dip fillets into batter. Carefully lower battered fillets into 370°F oil. Cook until fillets are golden brown in colour. Drain on paper toweling. Serve with lemon tea.

WABIGOON WALLEYE AND BEER

4 half pound walleye fillets
4 tablespoons minced onion
5 tablespoons butter
3 tablespoons flour
2 tablespoons brown sugar
1 1/2 tablespoons lemon juice

3 teaspoons salt
1/2 teaspoon pepper
paprika
2 cups of beer
1 clove

Sprinkle and rub walleye fillets with salt, paprika and pepper. Slowly saute onions in frying pan with butter. Add flour until brown and slowly mix in beer until beer comes to a boil. Add fish to the brown sauce and include sugar and clove. Place lid partially on pan and cook for 25 minutes over slow heat. Remove fish and add lemon juice to sauce. Pour sauce over the walleye.

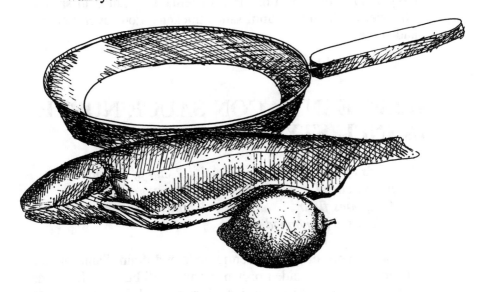

BLIND RIVER POACHED PICKEREL FILLETS

4 pickerel fillets
5 cups of dry white wine
1/3 cup butter
2 medium onions, minced
2 tablespoons salad oil
garlic powder to taste

1/2 teaspoon pepper
1/3 teaspoon salt
1/4 teaspoon tarragon
2 tablespoons flour
1 tablespoon tomato paste

Place all ingredients except the walleye, flour and butter in a skillet. Place the pickerel in this marinade and let soak for 3 to 4 hours. Bring marinade to a boil and then lower heat and simmer fish for 30 minutes. Without breaking fish, remove to a hot platter. Melt butter in a saucepan and stir in flour until silky. Add butter and flour mix to remaining sauce in skillet. Stir over medium heat until sauce thickens. Pour over pickerel and serve.

WALLEYE IN BACON SAUCE NORTH CHANNEL STYLE

4 pounds of walleye fillets
1/3 pound sliced & diced bacon
3 tablespoons flour
2 medium sized chopped onions

1 1/2 cup of boiling water
3 tablespoons vinegar
1 tablespoon lemon juice

Fry bacon until crisp and then remove and drain. Saute onions in bacon fat until golden brown. Remove all but 2 tablespoons of bacon grease. Stir in flour, cook and blend. Return bacon to pan with boiling water. Let simmer for a few minutes and then add vinegar and lemon juice. Place fillets in a well greased baking dish. Pour sauce over fish. Season with salt and pepper. Bake uncovered for 1 hour at 350°F.

YELLOW PERCH

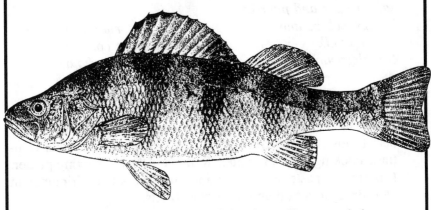

Rated as the tastiest of panfish, the yellow perch has a flesh that is white, flaky, firm and, best of all, delicious. Because the fish is easy to catch, the perch is an ideal target species for younger anglers. Perch can be baked, poached, pan-fried, deep-fried or barbecued.

GREAT LAKES YELLOW PERCH WITH CHEESE

2 pounds of perch fillets
1/2 teaspoon of salt
2 tablespoons apple juice
1/2 cup of cracker crumbs

1/2 cup of flour
pepper to taste
1 beaten egg
1/4 cup of grated cheese

Rinse fillets with fresh water and pat dry. Coat fillets with a mixture of flour and seasoning. Combine egg and apple juice. Dip floured fillets in this mixture. Combine crackers and cheese and roll the dipped fish in these crumbs. Fry in hot oil until golden brown.

MANITOU PERCH DELIGHT

10 to 12 medium sized perch fillets
salt, pepper and paprika
2 eggs well beaten
1/2 cup milk
5 tablespoons shortening

1/2 cup tomato paste
1 teaspoon cornstarch
3 tablespoons flour

Dip fish in egg and then roll in flour. Melt shortening and brown as many fillets at one time over medium heat. Reduce heat to low. Season fillets with salt, pepper and paprika. Continue cooking for 20 minutes. Remove fillets to serving platter. Mix tomato paste, cornstarch and milk and add to drippings in pan. Bring to a boil and pour over fillets.

TURKEY POINT BAKED PERCH FILLETS

3 pounds perch fillets
1 tablespoon flour
1 1/2 tablespoons butter
1 medium sized onion, minced
1 chicken bouillon cube dissolved in 1 cup of water

1/2 cup bread crumbs
1 teaspoon lemon juice
1/2 bay leaf
salt and pepper to taste

Spread perch fillets evenly in a greased baking dish. Melt butter in a bowl and stir in flour and onions. Add bouillon cube mixture and bay leaf. Stir and simmer for 15 minutes until mixture is thickened. Add lemon juice, salt and pepper. Remove bay leaf and continue stirring. Pour over fillets and sprinkle bread crumbs on top. Bake in a pre-heated oven for 20 minutes at 400°F.

POTTAWATOMI WRAPPED PERCH FILLETS

1 sheet puff pastry
8 perch fillets
pepper to taste
2 tablespoons butter

4 tablespoons mayonnaise
1/2 teaspoon lemon juice
1 egg yolk, lightly beaten

Cut pastry into 4, rolling each to an 8 inch square. Place a fillet on each pastry square. Mix pepper, lemon juice, mayonaise and butter together and put 1/4 of it on each fillet. Place second fillet on next (making a sandwich) and wrap pastry around, sealing it well. Brush pastry wrap with egg yolk. Bake, uncovered, at 400°F for 20 to 25 minutes. Serve as is piping hot, or top with your favorite sauce.

BASIC PAN FRIED PERCH

10 to 12 medium size perch fillets
2 eggs well beaten
1 cup of all purpose flour
1 teaspoon salt
1 teaspoon pepper

2 teaspoons milk
2 teaspoons cooking oil
1 cup corn meal

Cover each fillet thoroughly with a mixture of flour, salt and pepper. Toss fillets lightly from hand to hand to remove any excess flour. Dip floured fillets in mixture of eggs, oil and milk. Be certain all surfaces of the fillets are exposed to liquid mixture. Dredge the fillets in corn meal. Once again be sure all surfaces are covered with a light coating. Let fillets dry for 5 minutes on absorbent paper towels. Pan fry in a just foaming mixture of butter and cooking oil at a depth of 1/4 inch for 3 to 4 minutes on each side.

BUTTERMILK MIXTURE FOR PREVIOUS RECIPE

1/2 cup seasoned all-purpose flour
1/2 cup buttermilk   *1 cup cornmeal*

As before, dredge fillets in flour. Dip in buttermilk. Add cornmeal. Be certain no excess coating sticks to fish. Dry fillets for 5 minutes then cook.

APPLE BROILED POINT ABINO PERCH

2 pounds of perch fillets   *3/4 teaspoon salt*
3 tablespoons of melted margarine
3 teaspoons of apple juice

Sprinkle fillets of perch with salt. Brush with a mixture of apple juice and melted margarine. Broil for 10 minutes or until tender.

FAST FOIL BAKED PERCH

2 pounds perch fillets   *condensed canned milk*
1 cup fine ground bread crumbs

Dip fillets in condensed canned milk, then into bread crumbs. Lay on oiled aluminum foil and place in pre-heated oven at 350°F for 25 to 30 minutes. Garnish with lemon and parsley and serve hot.

LION'S HEAD PERCH FILLETS

2 pounds of perch fillets
1/2 cup of bread crumbs
1/2 cup of soft margarine
1 teaspoon prepared mustard

2 tablespoons of sour cream
1 teaspoon salt
3 tablespoons of apple juice
1/4 teaspoon pepper

Spread bread crumbs on bottom of greased baking pan. Arrange fillets on bottom of pan. Combine rest of ingredients in bowl and stir until smooth. Pour mixture over fillets, making certain that all are covered. Bake at 350°F until fillets are tender. Baste several times and serve hot.

LONG POINT PERCH IN BATTER

2 pounds of perch fillets
2/3 cup milk
1 teaspoon baking powder
1/2 teaspoon pepper
2 teaspoons prepared mustard

1 cup of flour
1 tablespoon cornstarch
1 teaspoon salt
2 eggs separated

Combine dry mixture. Mix egg yolk , milk and mustard. Stir into dry ingredients. Beat egg whites and fold in. Dredge fillets in flour and dip in batter. Cook in frying pan with approximately an inch of cooking oil. Drain perch and serve with horseradish.

KEN JAMIESON'S BROILED PERCH FILLETS

2 pounds of perch fillets
3 tablespoons of lemon juice
dash white pepper

1/4 cup of melted bacon fat
1 teaspoon of salt
paprika

Combine fat, lemon juice, salt and pepper. Place perch fillets on well greased broiler pan and brush with fat. Sprinkle with paprika. Broil about 3 inches from heat for 4 to 5 minutes. Turn and brush with fat. Sprinkle with paprika. Broil 4 to 5 minutes longer or until fish flakes easily . Serves 6 people.

SCALLOPED PERCH SURPRISE

2 cups of flaked cooked perch
2 cups white sauce
1/2 teaspoon pepper
3 tablespoons butter

2 tablespoons grated onion
1 teaspoon salt
1 cup bread crumbs

Into a buttered baking dish place in layers, 1/3 fish, 1/3 of seasoning and 1/3 of sauce. Repeat twice. Sprinkle buttered crumbs and bake at 350°F for 30 minutes.

OVEN CRUSTY PERCH

1 pound of perch fillets
3 teaspoons of salt
1 cup of Kellogg's Corn Flakes crumbs

1/2 cup of milk .
4 teaspoons of salad oil

Dip perch first into milk, then into crumbs. Arrange on well oiled baking sheet. Sprinkle fish with salad oil. Bake at 500°F for 15 minutes til tender. Serve with lemon or tartar sauce.

LITTLE CURRENT PERCH IN TOMATO DILL SAUCE

1 pound of perch fillets *1 cup chopped onions*
2 tablespoons butter *1 tablespoon flour*
1 can of condensed consomme *1/2 cup tomato catsup*
3/4 cup of sliced dill pickle

Heat oven to 450°F. Saute onions in butter. Stir in flour. Gradually add consomme and catsup. Simmer 25 minutes, stirring occasionally. Add pickles. Place fish in baking dish and cover with sauce. Bake 25 to 30 minutes or until fish flakes easily.

GORE BAY CHEESE AND BACON PERCH

3 fillets per person *barbecue sauce*
onion sliced rings *chives*
garlic powder *salt and pepper to taste*
grated mozzarella cheese *2 tablespoons butter*
1 cooked slice of bacon per fillet

Place each fillet on a small piece of heavy foil. Add bacon, onion ring, salt, pepper, garlic, butter and then cheese to fillet. Barbecue sauce and chives can be added if desired. Wrap securely. Cook over hot coals until desired flaking has been reached.

NORTHERN PIKE

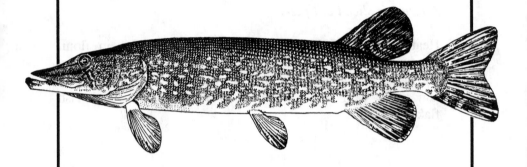

The little ones are often cursed and the big ones just pursued as trophies, but the Northern Pike can make for some mighty fine eating. Found throughout Canada, the American Midwest and Alaska, big fish generally inhabit big water. Release those lunker trophies to fight another day, but don't ever be afraid to keep a few of the little ones for table fare.

CHEESE TOPPED PIKE FILLETS

1 1/2 pounds pike fillets   *salt and pepper to taste*
1/2 cup mayonnaise   *1/2 cup shredded cheese*
1 egg white   *dash cayenne pepper*

Place fillets on broiler rack and sprinkle with salt and pepper. Broil about 4 inches from unit for 10 minutes. Combine mayonnaise, cayenne pepper and cheese. Beat egg white until stiff and fold into dressing. Spread on fish and broil until puffed and lightly browned. Serves 6.

BAKED PIKE WITH HAM

4 pounds northern pike *1/4 cup chopped onion*
3/4 pounds chopped ham *1 1/2 cups bread croutons*
1/4 cup vegetable oil *1/2 teaspoon thyme*
salt and pepper to taste

Take everything but the pike and mix. Clean the cavity of the pike and wipe with a fine coating of butter or oil. Fill cavity of pike with dressing and close with toothpicks. Drape 5 or 6 strips of bacon over fish. Place in roasting pan and bake for 30 to 35 minutes at 350°F. White wine can be added to bottom of roasting pan before baking if desired.

ENGLISH DEEP BATTERED PIKE

6 good-sized pike fillets or a dozen little ones
2 cups flour *2 teaspoons salt*
2 eggs, separated *1 cup lukewarm water*
2 tablespoons shortening

Wash fillets, rinse and pat dry. Beat egg whites until stiff. Combine egg yolks, flour, salt and baking powder and mix with water and melted shortening. Beat and fold in egg whites. Immerse pike fillets in batter, draining off excess. Slowly lower into hot deep fryer (375°F) for 3 to 5 minutes. There should be enough batter for 2 or 3 pounds of pike.

FAST BUT TASTY PIKE STICKS

3 pounds pike fillets　　　　*1 egg, well beaten*
1 cup flour　　　　　　　　 *1 cup cornmeal*

Clean fish and remove all bones and skin. Cut pike into portions (sticks) 2 inches long and 1 inch wide. Dip each stick into beaten egg and then roll it in cornmeal and flour mix. Fry in hot fat for 2 to 3 minutes. Salt and pepper to taste.

RED BAY ROLLED PIKE

3 pounds pike　　　　　　　*1 envelope sour cream mix*
1/2 cup mayonnaise　　　　 *2 teaspoons minced onion*

Use package to prepare sour cream. Mix mayonnaise, sour cream and onions. Roll pike fillets and hold with toothpicks. Place fish in a well-greased pan. Pour sour cream mix over fish. Bake at 350°F for 20 minutes. Serve with lemon.

CREAMED PIKE

1 cup flaked pike　　　　　 *1 cup milk*
salt and pepper to taste　　 *1 tablespoon flour*
2 tablespoons melted margarine

Break pike onto small flakes, removing any bones. Mix pike with melted butter and warm in small cooking pot. In a separate bowl, mix flour with a spoonful of water, then add milk. Pour mixture over pike. Add salt and pepper and cook until boiling.

Serve the above recipe over slices of hot buttered toast. The result: an old English recipe for finnan haddie.

NORTHERN ONTARIO PIKE PATTIES

2 cups cooked pike   *2 tablespoons margarine*
1/2 cup cracker crumbs   *2 eggs*
1/2 cup chopped onion   *1 tablespoon lemon juice*
3 drops of hot sauce or paprika

Fry onions lightly in butter. Flake pike and mix with onions, eggs, lemon juice, cracker crumbs, salt and hot sauce. Form into patties. Fry in margarine until browned. Serve with lemon slices.

DR. BILL JOHNSTON'S BAKED NORTHERN FILLETS

pike fillets   *flour*
1 egg   *cornflake crumbs*
salt and pepper   *lemon juice*

Line a cookie sheet with foil and rub it generously with butter. Dip each serving of fillet successively in flour, beaten egg and cornflake crumbs and place on foil. Then sprinkle generously with salt and pepper. Place in a 425°F oven for 15 minutes. Remove from oven and dribble melted butter on each fillet and sprinkle with lemon juice. Return to a 375°F oven and bake for 15 to 20 minutes more.

It is not necessary to turn the fillets when you bake them this way. Lower the temperature until you are ready to serve the fish. Leftover fillets may be frozen and later reheated in oven or broiler.

PARRY SOUND PIKE PUFFS

2 cooked, flaked pike
2 cups mashed potatoes
1 teaspoon paprika

3 eggs
3/4 cup milk
salt, pepper to taste

Thoroughly mix milk, salt, pepper, paprika, 2 eggs and pike in bowl. Form tablespoon-size balls. Bake at 350°F for 15 minutes. Beat remaining egg to a froth. Pour egg over pike and bake until golden.

STURGEON BAY PIKE SALAD

2 pounds cooked, flaked pike
4 tablespoons salad oil

2 cups chopped celery
2 tablespoons vinegar

Place fish in salad bowl. Mix oil and vinegar and pour over fish. Add celery to fish. Arrange lettuce leaves in cup shape. Fill with fish mix. Add spoonful of mayonnaise to top of each fish serving.

FRIED PIKE ITALIAN STYLE

3 pounds of pike fillets
3 eggs
1/2 teaspoon garlic salt
1/2 teaspoon Italian seasoning

1/2 cup flour
5 tablespoons water
1/2 teaspoon oregano
salt, pepper, garlic to taste

Combine egg with water, garlic, salt, oregano, Italian seasoning and pepper. Mix well. Dip fillets in this mixture and then drop into a bag of flour. Shake well to coat pike. Fry pike in hot peanut oil until brown. Serve with lemon.

LITE PIKE DELIGHT

3 pounds of pike fillets   *2 cans of stewed tomatoes*
1 medium diced green pepper   *1 medium diced onion*

Place pike in well greased baking dish. Pour tomatoes over pike. Layer onion, pepper over tomatoes. Sprinkle salt and pepper over onion. Bake in oven at 350°F for 30 minutes.

LAKE SIMCOE BROILED NORTHERN

one 5 pound pike   *3 tablespoons butter*
3 teaspoons lemon juice   *1 cup dry wine*
5 teaspoons water   *salt, pepper to taste*
2 teaspoons flour

Split pike lengthwise. Place in well greased broiling pan with the skin side down. Sprinkle pike with salt, pepper and lemon juice. Spread fish with butter. Place pike under broiler 6 inches from flame. Broil 15 minutes or until fish flakes. Baste frequently with wine, and lemon juice.

SIX MILE BAY PICKLED PIKE

2 quarts raw cubed pike   *3 quarts water*
2 cups sugar   *4 medium sliced onions*
4 teaspoons pickling spices   *1 1/2 cups pickling salt*

Place pike, cold water and pickling salt in gallon glass container. Refrigerate for 48 hours. Rinse pike in cold water. Add sugar, onions and spices to glass jar. Add pike. Cover with vinegar.

GRAND RIVER PIKE WITH EGG SAUCE

3 pounds pike
1-1/2 cups hot fish stock
2 tablespoons flour

2 beaten egg yolks
3 tablespoons butter

Clean pike and boil in salted water for 25 minutes. Reserve 1-1/2 cups of fish stock. Add melted butter and flour to stock. Add egg yolks. Stir thoroughly. Pour over hot pike and season to taste.

KEY RIVER PIKE CHOWDER

2 pounds pike fillets
1/3 cup chopped onions
1/3 cup chopped green peppers
1 can of corn
2 teaspoon salt
1 minced clove of garlic

7 slices bacon
4 cups milk
1 1/2 cup diced potatoes
5 hard boiled eggs
1/4 teaspoons pepper
3 tablespoons parsley

Fry bacon in pan. Save bacon grease. Drain and crumble bacon. Cook onions, pepper, garlic in bacon drippings until tender. In soup pot, add 1/2 cup of water and cook pike until tender. Remove pike and flake. Into remaining broth add milk, bacon bits, onions, salt, pepper, garlic, cooked potatoes, fish, corn and other seasoning. cook for 5 minutes. Serve with French bread.

MUSKELLUNGE

King of North American game fish, the musky is also tasty fresh from the pan or the oven. Many believe that the musky carries too fishy a taste, but this can be remedied by filleting when pan or deep frying. Lake of the Woods, Eagle Lake, Georgian Bay and the Kawartha Lakes in Canada, as well as Lake St. Clair, the St. Lawrence River and many of the lakes and rivers in Wisconsin and Minnesota offer world-class musky angling.

* Some angling fraternities such as Muskies Unlimited and Muskies Canada believe that the musky should be fished only for sport and then released. Still, not all fish can be released and should not be wasted. For those who enjoy the taste of musky these recipes will assist you in the kitchen.

BATH LUNGE AND BEER FRY

3 pounds of musky fillets
3 cups of pancake flour
2 teaspoons salt
1/2 teaspoon garlic

2 cups of beer
3 eggs
1 teaspoon pepper

Mix pancake flour, salt, pepper, garlic and beer. Include eggs and mix vigorously to a smooth batter. Cover fish with batter, shake off excess batter. Fry in hot peanut oil. Serve with lemon wedges.

MELODY BAY MUSKY BAKE

4 pounds lunge fillets
1/2 cup flour
shortening or butter

2 eggs
2 cups fine bread crumbs
salt and pepper to taste

Beat eggs. Dip fillets in flour and shake off excess. Dip fillets in egg and shake off excess. Roll in bread crumbs, covering fillets completely. Brown both sides of fish in hot frying pan for 30 to 60 seconds. Place musky fillets in preheated 400°F oven. Bake for 10 minutes. Remove and serve with tea and lemon slices.

STONEY LAKE MUSKY FILLETS OVER COALS

4 pounds lunge fillets
2 small cans mushrooms
2 teaspoons garlic salt

1 pound butter
2 tablespoons oregano

Slice musky fillets into finger portions. Lay out on aluminum foil. Position slices of butter over and around fish. The same with mushrooms, oregano, garlic, salt and pepper. Place over charcoal or in oven at 350°F for 30 minutes. Serve with corn on the cob, white wine or beer.

ST. LAWRENCE BALLED MUSKY

2 pounds of flaked musky
2 cups of bread crumbs

1/4 cup milk
salt, pepper, garlic

Salt and pepper fish. Drown bread crumbs in milk. Squeeze extra milk out and mix in musky. Deep fry golden brown.

PENATANGUISHENE STUFFED LUNGE

3 tablespoons minced onion   *1/4 cup butter*
3/4 cup chopped mushrooms   *5 pound lunge*
2 1/2 cups soft bread crumbs

Brown onions and mushrooms in butter. Combine with bread crumbs. Clean lunge by wiping out cavity, removing head and fins. Stuff with dressing and tie cavity closed. Pour 1/4 cup water into bake pan (lemon juice can be added if desired). Bake lunge at 350°F for one hour or until flaky.

COUCHICHING MUSKELLUNGE FILLETS

1 tablespoon worcestershire sauce
5 or 6 musky fillets   *1/2 cup margarine*
1 tablespoon lemon juice   *1 tablespoon vinegar*
1 teaspoon prepared mustard   *1/2 teaspoon pepper*
1 teaspoon salt

Place fillets in shallow baking dish which has been previously layered with bread crumbs. Cover fillets with sauce made from the above ingredients. Garnish with paprika and bake at 475°F allowing 10 minutes per inch of fillet.

HUNGRY MAN'S MUSKY STEW

3 pounds potatoes   *1 1/2 pounds musky fillets*
salt and pepper to taste   *cayenne pepper*
bacon slices

Place in baking dish layers of musky alternated with layers of potatoes, ending with a layer of potatoes on top. After each layer allow a light brushing of margarine, salt and pepper. Over the top arrange slices of fat bacon. Sprinkle with cayenne pepper. Pour in enough water to cover, and bake with cover on at 250°F until tender. Near the end, remove cover and let the top brown.

KAWARTHA MUSKY IN BEER

3 pounds of musky fillet chunks
1 bottle of beer   *3 egg yolks*

Cut musky fillets into 3 inch pieces. Place fish in medium sized Dutch oven. Cover musky with beer. Season with mixture of salt, pepper, and garlic. Beat egg yolks. Simmer musky until tender. Remove fish from Dutch oven. Add egg yolks to beer mix. Stir till smooth. Pour over musky and serve with lemon slices.

STONEY LAKE MUSKY SPECIAL

3 pounds of musky fillets   *2 cups of flour*
4 eggs   *6 tablespoons of flat beer*
5 tablespoons Parmesan cheese *salt and pepper to taste*

Mix cheese, salt, eggs and flour. Add beer and stir until smooth. Roll fillets in flour then batter. Deep fry until golden.

MOIRA LAKE MUSKY AND TOMATO

2 pounds of musky fillets
1 can tomato juice
salt, pepper to taste
pinch of parsley

3 green onions
1 lemon
1/4 teaspoon basil

Place musky fillets in well buttered baking dish. Cut green onions into pieces and sprinkle on top of musky. Add salt, basil and parsley. Pour tomato juice over fish just to cover. Bake at 350°F for 30 minutes. Garnish with lemon wedges.

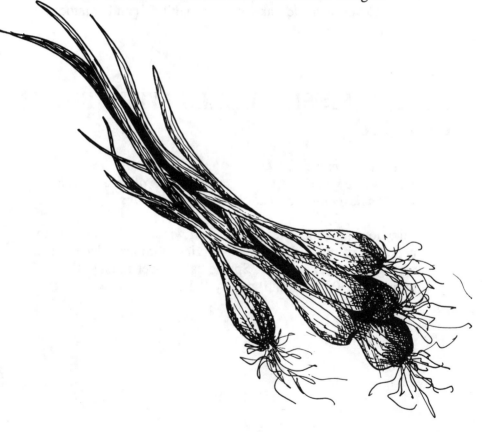

ONTARIO FISHERMAN MUSKY STEW

3 pounds of musky
8 bacon slices
1 teaspoon pepper

3 pounds of potatoes
1 teaspoon salt

Peel and slice potatoes in 1/4 inch silver dollars. In to a well greased baking dish, layer musky and potatoes, ending with potatoes on top. Cover each layer of potatoes with a generous amount of butter. On top of potatoes lay out fat bacon slices. Sprinkle top with salt and pepper mix. Add water to cover top layer. Cover dish and bake at 300°F until fish and potatoes are tender.

MADOC MUSKY BALLS WITH BLUE CHEESE

2 pounds of musky fillets
1 cup white wine
1 1/4 tablespoon chopped chives

1 1/4 cup sour cream
3 ounces of blue cheese
2 tablespoons flour

Mix flour and sour cream. Blend in wine, chives, cheese and pepper. Cut musky into small serving portions. Place fish in well greased baking dish. Spread sauce over musky. Bake 30 minutes at 300°F or until musky flakes.

LAKE TROUT

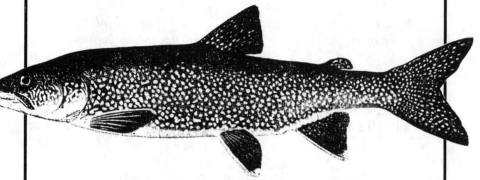

A creature of the deep, lake trout often reside in depths of 100 feet or more during the summer months. Wire line or downriggers are the best means of taking a lure down to these fish.

As table fare, there is no better member of the char family to dine on. Lake trout can be baked, poached, deep-fried, boiled or smoked. The deep lakes of the Northwest Territories, the Great Lakes and high waters of Montana offer world-class fishing for lake trout.

MEAFORD LAKE TROUT IN WINE

5 six-ounce trout steaks *1/2 cup red wine*
1/4 teaspoon marjoram *1/2 teaspoon onion powder*
1/16 teaspoon pepper *seasoning salt to taste*

Set lake trout in shallow greased pan. Mix wine, onion powder, marjoram and pepper. Pour liquid over trout. Place in refrigerator for 5 hours, turning fish on the hour. Remove and drain well. Grill fish, turning once, until trout flakes easily with fork.

MANITOU GRILLED LAKER STEAKS

4 pound lake trout steaks 1 inch thick
2 tablespoons finely chopped onion
2 teaspoons grated lemon rind   1/2 teaspoon marjoram
6 tablespoons lemon juice   1/2 cup salad oil
1 teaspoon salt   1/4 teaspoon pepper

Arrange fish steaks in shallow pan. Mix ingredients and pour over fish. Marinate steaks for 1 hour, turning once. Place fish in a greased, hinged wire grill about 4 inches from coals. Cook 8 to 10 minutes on each side. Great with tartar sauce and beer.

GEORGIAN ISLAND LAKE TROUT AND CHEESE

4 pounds fresh lake trout fillets   1 teaspoon salt
1/4 teaspoon pepper   6 cups soft bread cubes
12 tablespoons bacon fat   2 cups chopped onions
2 teaspoons dried mustard   1/2 cup chopped parsley
2 cups grated cheddar cheese

Season fillets with salt and pepper and arrange in greased baking pan. Toast bread cubes. Melt butter and add onions, cooking until brown. Stir in mustard and bread cubes with butter and onion mixture. Add cheese and parsley. Toss until well mixed. Spread topping over fillets. Bake fish for 20 minutes at 350°F.

BAKED GEORGIAN BAY SPLAKE

2 to 4 pound hybrid lake trout
1/4 cup melted butter
4 tablespoons lemon juice
paprika

oregano
celery salt
basil

Lay clean fish in greased baking dish and rub with lemon juice, butter and other ingredients. Bake for approximately 20 minutes at 350°F.

MINDEMOYA BAKED LAKE TROUT

5 pound lake trout
1/4 cup melted butter
1 teaspoon paprika

2 cups sour cream
chopped parsley

Split and remove bones from lake trout. Rub inside and out of fish with paprika and butter. Place in large oven dish. Cover with sour cream. Place lid on dish and bake for 45 minutes at 400°F.

LAKE OF THE WOODS BAKED LAKE TROUT

4 pound filleted lake trout
2 diced medium-sized onions
salt and pepper to taste

4 chopped tomatoes
1 1/2 cups corn flakes

Season lake trout fillets with salt and pepper. Arrange fillets in greased baking dish. Mix onions, corn flakes, tomato and 1/4 cup of water. Pour mixture over fish. Add dabs of butter and a sprinkling of paprika. Bake in oven at 350°F for 30 minutes.

LAKE OF BAYS BAKED GREY TROUT

1 5 pound lake trout   *4 tablespoons butter*
3/4 cup diced onion   *1 cup table cream*
1 teaspoon grated lemon rind   *salt and pepper to taste*
paprika to taste

Clean, wash and wipe lake trout. Place trout in a well buttered baking pan. In a saucepan saute onions in the remaining butter. Add pepper, salt, lemon rind and small amount of flour. Stir cream in slowly. Heat sauce to a simmer and then pour over trout. Sprinkle fish with paprika. Bake in preheated oven at 400°F for 25 to 30 minutes.

LAKE OF THE WOODS ALMOND TROUT

2 pounds of lake trout fillets *1/3 cup of vegetable oil*
4 tablespoons milk   *1 cup of cracker crumbs*
1/3 cup of flour   *1/2 cup sliced almonds*
3 tablespoons melted butter   *1 egg*

Mix flour and pepper in small bowl. In another bowl blend egg and milk. Mix cracker crumbs and almonds on wax paper. First roll fish in flour. Drain off excess and dip in egg mix. Finally coat with almond/cracker mix. Place fish in small baking pan that has been greased with oil and margarine. Baste trout lightly with oil and arrange in pan. Bake at 400 to 450°F in oven for 7 to 10 minutes. Serve with lemons.

SIOUX LOOKOUT BAKED LAKE TROUT

6 to 8 pound lake trout　　　*1/2 cup barbecue sauce*
1 lemon　　　*1/2 cup butter*
1 tablespoon worcestershire sauce

Combine barbecue sauce, juice of the lemon, worcestershire sauce and butter. Heat and mix in small saucepan. Clean trout, remove scales and split along backbone to remove backbone. Leave skin on fish. Place fish on well greased rack. Place similar rack on opposite side of trout. Place trout on hot barbecue. Grill 2 to 3 inches above coals. Cook 10 to 15 minutes with flesh side towards coals. Turn fish over. Baste fish with sauce. Cook fish an additional 10 to 15 minutes.

OWEN SOUND LAKE TROUT STEAK DELIGHT

6 six-ounce lake trout steaks　　　*1/2 cup salad oil*
1/4 cup parsley　　　*1/4 cup lemon juice*
2 tablespoons grated onion　　　*1/2 teaspoon dry mustard*
1/4 teaspoon salt　　　*1/4 teaspoon pepper*

Place trout steaks in a shallow bowl. Combine all remaining ingredients, mix well and pour over trout steaks. Place in refrigerator for 1 hour. Remove turn steaks and then return to refrigerator for another hour. Place trout over a well greased barbecue rack. Grill over medium hot coals until fish is lightly browned. Baste with marinade and then turn on coals. Cook for 6 to 8 minutes longer or until fish flakes. Serve with lemon wedges.

DAVEY ISLAND LAKE TROUT LOAF WITH SHRIMP

3 cups of flaked, cooked trout
1 cup rolled oats
2 tablespoons flour
2 tablespoons minced parsley
1 10 ounce can of shrimp soup

1 1/2 cups milk
2 tablespoons melted butter
1/2 teaspoon salt
2 beaten eggs

Sprinkle lake trout with lemon juice. Melt butter in frying pan and stir in flour until thick and smooth. Stir in milk, salmon, eggs, salt, parsley and rolled oats. Pour mixture into well greased 9 inch baking pan. Bake in preheated 350°F oven for 30 minutes. Heat shrimp soup in double boiler and when ready pour over fish loaf.

NORTH CHANNEL LAKE TROUT BURGERS

2 cups flaked, cooked trout
1/4 cup vegetable oil
2 beaten eggs
1/3 cup mayonnaise
1 teaspoon powdered mustard
1 tablespoon chopped sweet pickle

1/2 cup minced onions
2/3 cup bread crumbs
1/4 cup parsley flakes
6 buttered hamburger rolls

Saute onions in vegetable oil. Add lake trout, bread crumbs, eggs, eggs, parsley, mustard, and salt. Form into burgers. Fry trout burgers in hot oil for 3 minutes on each side until golden brown. Combine mayonnaise and pickle. Place trout burgers on bottom of roll. Top each with 1 tablespoon of mayonnaise mix.

HICKORY-BROILED LAKE TROUT STEAKS

Hickory Sauce

1/2 cup catsup

3 tablespoons lemon juice

1 tablespoon Hickory smoke

1 teaspoon Worcestershire sauce

1 teaspoon powdered mustard

1 tablespoon soy sauce

1/4 cup salad oil

2 tablespoons vinegar

1 teaspoon salt

3 drops Tabasco sauce

1/4 teaspoon celery salt

1 garlic clove, chopped

Combine all ingredients and mix well. Makes about 1 1/2 cups.

6 trout steaks, 6 to 8 ounces each

2 tablespoons salt

1 cup water

Place trout in a shallow pan. Mix salt and water and pour over steaks; soak in salt solution for 3 minutes. Place steaks in clean pan. Pour sauce over steaks; marinate for 30 minutes. Charcoal broil or oven broil steaks 8 to 10 minutes, or until fish is lightly browned on 1 side; baste with sauce. Turn steak and broil 5 minutes longer or until flesh flakes easily; baste with sauce. Serve remaining marinade sauce with steaks. Serves 6.

NORTH BAY LAKE TROUT TARRAGON

1 trout, 3 pounds
1/2 cup tarragon wine vinegar
4 peppercorns
pepper to taste

2 cups water
1 tablespoon onion, minced
salt to taste
parsley sprigs to garnish

Clean trout; wrap in cheesecloth and place on rack in large kettle. Combine next 6 ingredients and pour over fish. Cover and simmer 45 minutes. Lift fish out carefully; remove skin. Serve either hot or well chilled. Decorate platter with parsley. Top salmon with spoonfuls of Tarragon Sauce. Serves 6.

TARRAGON SAUCE

1 cup sour cream
pepper to taste
1/2 teaspoon sugar
2 tablespoons tarragon wine vinegar

salt to taste
1 tablespoon cut scallions

Combine all ingredients and mix thoroughly. Makes 1 cup.

SIMPLE LAKE TROUT SOUFFLE

2 cups trout, cooked and flaked
3 tablespoons butter, melted
1 cup evaporated milk
4 eggs, separated

3 tablespoons flour
1/4 teaspoon salt

Preheat oven to 350°. Remove skin and bones, and flake. Melt butter in a saucepan over low heat; gradually add flour and milk until thickened. Add salt. Remove from heat and stir in slightly beaten egg yolks; cook gently for another minute; remove from heat. Stir in flaked fish. Pour the cooked mixture into stiffly beaten egg whites, and fold. Pour into a buttered 2-quart baking dish and bake for 45 to 50 minutes. Serves 6.

BROOK TROUT

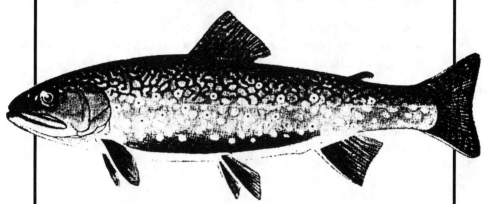

The brookie is famed as a fly fisher's delight, but this colorful creature will readily attack a micro spinner or small spoon. American anglers find brook trout in the clear streams of Maine, the Appalachian Mountains, Wisconsin, Minnesota and Michigan. The brook trout is also a favorite with Canadian anglers in Labrador, Quebec, Ontario and the Atlantic Provinces.

NORTH BAY SPECKLED TROUT CASSEROLE

2 to 3 pounds of brook trout fillets
1 cup of bread crumbs   *1/2 cup melted butter*
1/8 teaspoon prepared mustard   *1 tablespoon lemon juice*
1 tablespoon vinegar   *1 teaspoon salt*

Cover the bottom of a well greased baking dish with bread crumbs. Arrange trout fillets in dish. With remaining ingredients make a sauce. Pour over fish. Bake in a preheated 400°F oven for 20 minutes, basting occasionally with sauce.

SHINING TREE BACON WRAPPED BROOKIES

4 fresh brook trout
4 tablespoons chopped onion   *4 tablespoons melted butter*
4 strips of bacon   *salt and pepper to taste*

Stuff each trout with 1/4 of the onion and butter. Wrap each trout with one strip of bacon. Secure with toothpick. Salt and pepper to taste. Broil each side under medium heat for less than 10 minutes.

FAST-COOKED BROOK TROUT OVER CHARCOAL

4 small brook trout   *1/8 cup melted butter*
salt and pepper to taste

Place trout over charcoal grill. Turn frequently, basting with butter inside and out. Add salt and pepper.

HEARST BROOK TROUT BAKE

6 brook trout   *1 cup water*
1 1/2 cup dry wine   *worcestershire sauce*
1 cup butter   *salt and pepper to taste*

Clean and prepare fish for baking. Leave heads and tails on. Cover the bottom of a small roasting pan with butter. Mix wine, water, salt, pepper and worcestershire sauce. Arrange trout in roasting pan. Pour butter evenly and generously over fish. Pour wine mix over fish. Bake for 50 minutes at 340°F.

ALBANY RIVER STEAMED TROUT

4 good-sized brookies   *4 slices bacon*
1/2 stick of butter   *4 large onions*
water as required

Arrange brook trout in frying pan and add water until trout are half covered. Cook over medium heat with lid on pan, steaming fish. Add water as needed to maintain level. *Do not allow to fry!* Fry bacon until crisp. Melt butter in another frying pan. Add chopped onion. Crumble bacon and add to butter and onion. When skin begins to peel, discard it. Remove water and cover fish with butter mixture. Return lid and allow water to simmer for 2 to 5 minutes.

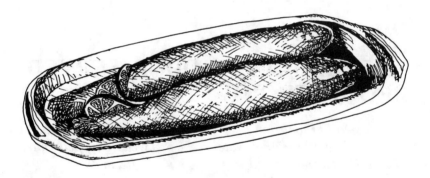

GOWGANDA SPECKLED TROUT SURPRISE

6 medium-sized brook trout
6 dashes lemon pepper
1 cup white wine
1/2 cup seafood seasoning
1 1/4 cup Bisquick

6 slices chopped bacon
2 teaspoons onion flakes
2 tablespoons of butter
1/2 cup coarse salt

In moderately hot skillet, heat the lemon pepper, bacon and onion flakes until bacon is cooked. Mix Bisquick, seafood seasoning and salt together in a plastic bag. Wet brook trout and shake in seasoning bag until trout is evenly covered. Place all 6 trout in skillet. Cover and cook for approximately 8 minutes. Turn trout and add butter and wine to skillet. Cover and cook for 7 minutes.

MAKOKIBATAN LODGE SERVED BROOK TROUT

6 small brook trout
2 1/2 teaspoons hot water
1 1/2 teaspoons salt
1/4 cup chopped green onions
1 teaspoon green olives

1 cup uncooked wild rice
1/3 cup chopped water
    chestnuts
4 tablespoons melted
    butter

Use a 3 quart saucepan to boil water, salt and rice. Stir and reduce heat once boiling point is reached. Cover and simmer for 50 minutes. In a small skillet cook water chestnuts, olives, butter, and green onions for approximately 3 minutes. Add rice to mix. Arrange brook trout in a well greased 13" X 9" baking dish. Stuff trout with rice mix. Brush fish evenly with melted butter. Bake for 20 minutes at 375°F.

ALGONQUIN PARK BROOK TROUT AND SHRIMP

5 brook trout
1 1/4 cup milk
1 egg yolk
1/4 teaspoon oregano
1/8 teaspoon hot sauce
5 ozs. of cooked and peeled shrimp
1/4 cup of uncooked chopped bacon
1/4 teaspoon worcestershire sauce

4 cups of bread crumbs
2 eggs
1/3 cup of diced onion
2 tablespoons lemon juice
1/4 teaspoon parsley

Split and de-bone trout. Leave head on fish. Add milk to bread crumbs. Squeeze dry. Mix in eggs. Cook bacon and onions. Include shrimp and saute for 7 minutes. Include bread and all other ingredients. Divide stuffing evenly into cavities of all trout. Close cavity with tooth picks. Place in preheated 400°F oven for 20 minutes. Baste occasionally with melted butter. Serve with lemon wedges.

PEMBROKE BAKED BROOK TROUT DELMONICO

3 pounds of brook trout fillets
3 tablespoons of lemon juice
1 1/2 teaspoons grated onions
1/8 teaspoon liquid hot pepper sauce
chopped parsley

1/3 cup melted butter
1 teaspoon salt
pepper to taste

Place brook trout fillets in well greased baking pan. Combine butter, lemon juice, onion and other seasonings. Pour over trout and bake in preheated oven at 350°F for 25 minutes.

PETAWAWA BAKED TROUT WITH SEAFOOD SAUCE

4 medium size brook trout
1/2 cup sweet pickled relish
1 teaspoon seafood seasoning
salt and pepper to taste

1 cup mayonnaise
1 medium grated onion
butter

Place mayonnaise, relish, onion and seafood seasoning in bowl and mix well. Refrigerate sauce until ready. Butter shiny side of aluminium foil. Arrange trout on foil and dot each with butter. Wrap trout in foil and bake in preheated oven at 450°F for 15 minutes. Serve with seafood sauce.

BROOK TROUT HUNTSVILLE STYLE

4 to 5 medium size brook trout
1 cup bean sprouts
8 to 10 strips of bacon
1/3 pound of diced mushrooms
2 medium sliced green onion

4 eggs
3/4 cup green peppers
2 teaspoons soy sauce
1 diced celery stalk
3 tablespoons cooking oil

In a heavy skillet heat oil, mushroom, bean sprouts, celery, green pepper, onions for 3 to 4 minutes over low heat. Add egg and soy sauce and continue to mix over low heat. Once eggs have stiffened stuff mixture into the cavity of each trout. Wrap trout bacon strips and close with toothpicks. Bake for 10 to 12 minutes at 450°F. Lemon juice can be sprinkled over trout halfway through baking cycle.

BARRY'S BAY SESAME TROUT

6 pan dressed brook trout   *1/4 cup of melted bacon fat*
1/4 cup of sesame seeds   *2 tablespoons lemon juice*
salt and pepper to taste

Clean, wash and dry trout. Combine remaining ingredients .
Place trout in well-greased hinged wire grill. Baste fish with
sauce. Cook 4 inches from broiler flame or barbecue coals for
5 minutes. Baste with sauce and then turn fish and cook for an
additional 4 minutes.

TEMAGAMI TROUT IN TOMATO SAUCE

6 or 8 small brook trout fillets   *1/2 lemon*
1/4 cup melted butter   *1/2 cup flour*
1 10 ounce can of condensed Campbell's tomato soup

Melt butter in an 8 inch square baking dish. Roll fillets in
flour. Arrange brook trout fillets in baking dish. Pour undiluted
tomato soup over fish. Squeeze juice of 1/2 lemon over tomato
soup. Bake for 25 minutes in preheated 350°F oven.

CAMPER'S ONION & TROUT FOIL

4 trout   *3/4 pounds butter*
1 package onion soup mix

Clean and wipe trout. Place each trout in separate foil. Prepare
a soup mix by melting butter and adding dry soup. Pour mixture evenly over all four trout. Seal fish tightly and rest over
coals for 10 to 15 minutes.

STEELHEAD

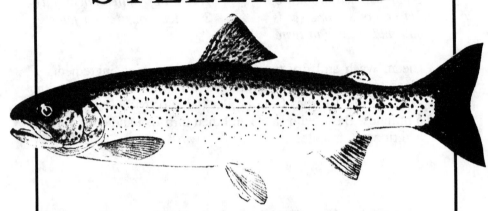

This wonderful sport fish has been transplanted from the Pacific Northwest to the Great Lakes. The steelhead or rainbow trout is best kept for the table when captured from the open water of the Pacific or the Great Lakes. Recent arrivals to spawning streams also make great meals. Steelhead that have been in the river long, tend to be soft of flesh and lose much of the table quality.

SOUTHAMPTON SUNSHINE STEELHEAD FILLETS

3 pounds steelhead fillets   *1/2 cup melted butter*
1 can orange juice concentrate   *salt and nutmeg to taste*

Place steelhead fillets skin side down in a single layer on a well-greased, shallow baking pan. Thaw orange juice concentrate and combine with butter and seasoning. Pour sauce over fillets. Bake at 350°F for 20 to 30 minutes.

BIGHEAD RIVER SPECIAL

2 cups flaked, cooked steelhead   12 slices bread
4 tablespoons chopped onion   butter
1/6 cup mayonnaise   2 tablespoons lemon juice
dash of worcestershire sauce

Remove any bones from flaked steelhead. Mix steelhead with worcestershire sauce, lemon juice, onion and salad dressing or mayonnaise. Spread mixture on 6 bread slices. Butter outside of the sandwiches and grill until toasted.

An excellent recipe for leftover trout.

PAN FRIED SAUBLE RIVER STEELHEAD

2 pounds steelhead   1 egg, beaten
2 tablespoons lemon juice   salt and pepper to taste
1 cup fine bread crumbs

Mix egg, lemon juice, salt and pepper together. Dip pieces of fish into egg mixture, dripping off excess. Roll in bread crumbs. Fry until golden brown.

Variation: for a coating similar to that of Weiner Schnitzel, add 1/2 teaspoon of anchovy paste to the egg mixture.

OWEN SOUND BAKED RAINBOW TROUT

8 pound steelhead   6 tablespoons butter
1 cup chopped onions   1/2 teaspoon paprika
1 tablespoon grated lemon rind   1 1/2 cups cream
salt and pepper to taste

Arrange steelhead in well greased baking dish. In a separate pot, melt butter and simmer onions until tender. Add lemon rinds, salt, pepper and a small sprinkling of flour. Stir in cream slowly and heat to a simmering temperature. Pour evenly over fish and sprinkle on paprika. Bake in oven for 25 minutes at 350°F.

COLLINGWOOD STEELHEAD SURPRISE

6 medium sized rainbow trout steaks
2 onions, chopped   2 carrots, chopped
2 celery stalks, chopped   1/2 cup butter
1/2 cup dry wine   1/4 cup chopped parsley
2 cloves   1 tablespoon salt
6 peppercorns

In a pan large enough to poach the steelhead, sauté the onions, carrots and celery in butter until soft. Add wine, parsley, cloves, salt and peppercorns. Stir and add 2 quarts of water. Cover and simmer for 5 minutes. Uncover and add trout. Simmer covered for 10 minutes or until fish flakes easily when fork tested. Chill the trout in stock and serve with tartar sauce.

ZESTY MUSHROOM STUFFING

1/4 cup onion, minced   *1/4 cup celery, minced*
1/4 cup butter, melted   *1/4 teaspoon dillweed*
1 tablespoon parsley, minced   *1/4 teaspoon salt*
1/2 pound fresh mushrooms, sliced
2 cups crackers, coarsely crushed
1/4 teaspoon poultry seasoning

In a large skillet sauté onion and celery in butter until golden. Add mushrooms and cook for 3 minutes. Add remaining ingredients; mix well. Enough for 4- to 6-pound fish.

SAUTEED STEELHEAD STEAKS

6 medium sized steelhead steaks   *1/4 cup butter*
2 tablespoons prepared mustard   *1/4 cup apple cider*

Spread steelhead steaks with mustard. Melt butter in pan and add cider. Sauté steaks about 10 minutes for each side. Serve with lemon wedges.

BAKED RAINBOW WITH HERB BUTTER

2 to 2 1/2 pounds rainbow
1 garlic clove, minced or mashed
1 small onion, finely chopped
3 tablespoons parsley, minced
1/2 teaspoon sweet basil, crumbled
1/2 teaspoon freshly ground pepper

1/4 cup butter or margarine
2 tablespoons lemon juice
1 teaspoon salt

Preheat oven to 300°. Place rainbow fillet on a piece of heavy paper or foil, and cut around fish (paper keeps rainbow skin from sticking to rack); slide fish and paper onto rack of broiler pan. Blend together remaining ingredients; spread over fillet. Bake for 25 to 30 minutes, depending on thickness of fillet, or until fish flakes with a fork. Serves 8.

OWEN SOUND BAY STEELHEAD POTATO CHOWDER

1 15 1/2-ounce can steelhead
1 cup tomato juice
1 cup potatoes, cubed
4 tablespoons butter, melted
1 teaspoon salt
1/2 teaspoon worcestershire sauce
3 cups milk

2 cups water
1/2 cup onion, chopped
1 teaspoon celery salt
4 tablespoons flour
1 teaspoon dry mustard

Drain, flake and remove skin and bones from steelhead. Combine first 6 ingredients in a large kettle; cover and simmer for 40 minutes. In another saucepan melt butter; add flour, salt, mustard, and worcestershire sauce; mix until smooth. Add milk slowly and stir constantly; cook until mixture thickens; combine with trout mix. Stir well and serve hot. Serves 8.

CHINOOK SALMON

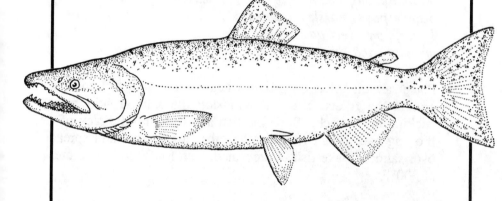

Native to the Pacific Northwest, the chinook salmon has been introduced to the Great Lakes, where it now ranks as a major game fish in lakes Superior, Michigan, Huron and Ontario. Not only an exciting sport fish, the chinook or king salmon also makes for delectable table fare.

HOT SALMON SALAD

Save that leftover baked salmon

lettuce
onion

tomato
salad dressing

Toss pieces of flaked salmon along with lettuce, tomato and onion in a bowl with some salad dressing. Heat until warmed and then serve with slices of hard-boiled eggs.

PORT ELGIN BAKED CHINOOK WITH HERB BUTTER

4 to 5 pounds king salmon fillets   *1/2 cup butter*
1 minced garlic clove   *2 teaspoons salt*
5 tablespoons lemon juice   *1 teaspoon pepper*
6 tablespoons parsley, minced
1 teaspoon sweet basil, crumbled
medium-sized onion finely chopped

Place salmon fillets on piece of heavy aluminum foil and cut around the fillets. The foil will stop the salmon skin from sticking to the rack. Slide the fish and foil onto the rack of a broiling pan. Blend together the other ingredients and spread over salmon. Bake fish in preheated oven for 20 to 25 minutes at 300°F.

SARNIA BREADED AND BAKED SALMON

8 to 10 pound king salmon   *5 teaspoons salt*
6 tablespoons butter   *1 1/2 teaspoons pepper*
1/2 cup chopped celery   *1 cup chopped onions*
1/2 cup chopped green peppers   *2 cups bread crumbs*
4 tablespoons white wine   *1 teaspoon thyme*
1/2 cup chopped mushrooms

Wash and dry whole fish. Wipe inside and out of salmon with 4 teaspoons of salt and 1 teaspoon of pepper. With half the butter, sauté the onions, peppers, celery and mushrooms for 10 minutes. Stir in bread crumbs, thyme, remaining pepper and salt. Carefully stuff fish and close with string. Place salmon in greased foil. Coat fish with remaining butter and wine. Close foil and bake at 400°F for 15 minutes. Open foil and bake for another 20 minutes, basting with butter once or twice.

THUNDER BAY CHINOOK SALMON BARBECUE

1 king salmon, 12 to 14 pounds   *salt to taste*
pepper to taste   *garlic salt to taste*

Split dressed salmon and remove backbone. Season split sides well with salt, pepper and garlic salt. Place cut sides down on oiled grill. After fire is hot, put on some green alder; when coals are glowing, place the grill about a foot above coals. Brown cut sides about 20 minutes; turn carefully; let cook 3 to 4 hours. Do not overcook. Serves 12 or more.

BAYFIELD POACHED CHINOOK AND SHRIMP

4 pounds of king fillets   *2 cups white wine*
pinch of thyme   *2 cups water*
1 bay leaf   *2 teaspoons salt*
4 cups strained fish stock   *4 tablespoons melted butter*
4 tablespoons flour   *4 slightly beaten egg yolks*
2 tablespoons lemon juice   *2 5-ounce cans of shrimp*
lemon slices   *paprika to garnish*

Wipe fillets and place in skillet with water, wine, bay leaf, thyme and salt. Bring to a fast boil, cover and simmer for 12 minutes. Drain fish, set stock aside. Melt butter and gradually stir in flour and fish stock, cooking until cream appears. Mix yolks, lemon juice and parsley and stir slowly onto sauce. Add drained shrimp and cook for 4 minutes. Put salmon on large platter and cover with sauce, and garnish with lemon wedges and paprika.

SAULT STE. MARIE KING SALMON CASSEROLE

3 pounds chinook salmon fillet	2 cups milk
4 eggs	2 large onions
2 cups cracker crumbs	2 green peppers
5 bay leaves	3 teaspoons salt

Wipe and cut fillets into small pieces. Chop peppers and onions into fine pieces. Combine all other ingredients and mix well. Place in casserole dish and bake for 1 hour at 350°F.

This will serve up to 8 hungry anglers.

OWEN SOUND SALMON WITH SOUR CREAM

3 pound chinook salmon	4 peppercorns
1/2 teaspoon seasoning salt	1/2 teaspoon celery salt
1/2 teaspoon shredded parsley	1 teaspoon salt
enough water to cover salmon	1 cup sour cream
1 teaspoon dillweed	1 tablespoon wine vinegar
1/4 teaspoon salt	

Mix sour cream, dillweed, wine vinegar and 1/4 teaspoon of salt to form sour cream sauce. Cool until ready for salmon. Clean chinook and place on rack in large kettle. Combine the rest of ingredients and pour over salmon. Cover and simmer in stock for 30 minutes. Carefully remove salmon to platter and serve either hot or cold with dillweed and sour cream sauce.

KINCARDINE CHINOOK PANCAKES

1 7 ounce jar of chinook salmon *1 cup of pancake mix*
1 egg *1 cup milk*
1 tablespoon salad oil

Combine all ingredients except salmon. Stir until smooth. Add salmon. Heat pancake griddle, oil lightly and fry each salmon pancake until golden brown. Serve with white sauce over pancakes.

SAUBLE BEACH SALMON STEAK DELIGHT

6 6 ounce salmon steaks *1/2 cup salad oil*
1/3 cup parsley *1/3 cup lemon juice*
2 tablespoons grated onion *1/3 teaspoon dry mustard*
salt and pepper to taste

Place chinook steaks in shallow baking bowl. Mix all other ingredients. Pour over steaks. Let stand for 2 hours. Place salmon on greased barbecue rack. Grill over hot coals for 4 to 6 minutes a side. Baste with marinade and turn. Barbecue for 4 to 6 more minutes. Serve with tartar sauce.

OSHAWA BROILED CHINOOK STEAKS

5 one-inch chinook steaks
4 tablespoons lemon juice
2 teaspoons grated lemon rind
1 1/2 tablespoons grated onion
1/4 cup of cooking oil
1/4 teaspoon marjoram
salt and pepper to taste

Place chinook steaks in well greased broiling pan. Mix all other ingredients and pour over chinook steaks. Marinade for 2 hours turning once. Drain and broil steaks 4 to 6 inches from heat for 10 minutes on each side.

POACHED CHINOOK STEAKS NORTH CHANNEL STYLE

4 king salmon steaks
1 sliced stalk of celery
1/2 cup of chicken broth
1 teaspoon dried dill
1 tablespoon chopped parsley
1 large sliced onion
1/2 cup dry white wine
1/4 teaspoon thyme
1/2 small bay leaf

Spread onion, herbs, celery in skillet. Arrange chinook steaks in single layer on top. Salt and pepper to taste. Pour wine and broth over fish. Bring to a boil, reduce heat and simmer with cover on for 10 minutes. Check fish to flake easily. Remove and serve with your favourite sauce.

POINT COMMODORE DEEP FRIED CHINOOK CHUNKS

one 15 to 20 pound salmon
2 cups milk
3 teaspoons salt
6 tablespoons baking powder

3 cups flour
4 eggs
corn or peanut oil
3 teaspoons garlic powder

To prepare batter, slowly mix flour, milk, baking powder, eggs, salt and garlic powder in large bowl. More milk can be added to reduce thickness. Fillet chinook into 2 inch chunks. Pour enough oil into large camp skillet to reach 1/2 to 1 inch level. Heat to a sizzle over hot coals. Dip fillets in batter and fry turning once. When golden brown, remove fillets and serve with lemon and vinegar.

OWEN SOUND BAY GOURMET SALMON STEAKS

4 pounds of salmon steaks
3/4 cup melted oil
2 tablespoons chopped chives
1 clove finely chopped garlic
1/4 teaspoon pepper
1/8 teaspoon sage
1/8 teaspoon liquid hot pepper sauce

1 cup dry vermouth
1/3 cup lemon juice
2 teaspoons salt
1/4 teaspoon marjoram
1/4 teaspoon thyme

Cut steaks in serving size portions. Place a single layer in a shallow baking dish. Combine remaining ingredients. Pour sauce over fish and let stand for four hours in refrigerator. Turn occasionally. Remove fish, reserving sauce for basting. Place fish in well-greased, hinged wire grills. Cook about 4 inches above moderately hot coals for 8 minutes. Baste with sauce. Turn and cook for 7 to 10 minutes longer or until fish flakes with fork. Serves 6 to 10.

LOMI LOMI ONTARIO CHINOOK

1 1/2 pounds fresh salmon   *lemon slices*
4 firm ripe medium tomatoes
3 finely chopped spring onions

This Hawaiian fish salad is described by the natives as ONO (delicious). De-bone and remove skin from salmon. Shred or dice fish. Place in bowl and chill. Dice tomatoes. Place in separate bowl and chill. Before serving, toss salmon and tomatoes together. Garnish with finely chopped onions. Place a few ice cubes in salad to keep it cool. If desired add lemon slices.

SYDENHAM RIVER CHINOOK MEUNIERE

3 pounds of salmon steaks   *1/4 cup flour*
1/2 teaspoons salt   *1/8 teaspoons pepper*
1/4 cup milk   *1/2 cup oil*
3 tablespoons butter   *juice of 1/2 lemon*
1 tablespoon parsley   *lemon slices*

Mix flour, salt and pepper. Dip salmon steaks in milk, then in flour mixture. Heat oil in large frying pan until sizzling hot. Add fish steaks one at a time and cook until golden brown. Heat butter in a small saucepan until it is brown. Remove fish to a platter and sprinkle with lemon juice, parsley and pour on browned butter over all. Garnish with lemon slices.

GRIFFITH ISLAND BAKED SALMON SALAD

2 pounds of leftover salmon
1 cup of thinly sliced celery
1/4 cup sliced pitted ripe olives
2 tablespoons French dressing
2 tablespoons salad dressing

2 cups of cooked rice
1/2 cup chopped parsley
1/2 cup mayonnaise
2 tablespoons lemon juice
1 teaspoon curry powder

Break salmon into large pieces. Combine rice, celery, parsley, olives and salmon. combine mayonnaise, French dressing, lemon juice, and curry powder. Add mayonnaise mixture to salmon mixture and toss lightly. Place in 6 well-greased 6 ounce casserole or custard cups. Top each with a teaspoons of mayonnaise. Sprinkle with paprika. Bake at 400°F in oven for 15 to 20 minutes or until heated.

PIER 89 SALMON CHOWDER

2 cups salmon cooked and flaked or one 15 1/2-ounce can
1 8-ounce can whole-kernel corn
1/4 cup butter, margarine, or bacon fat
1 cube chicken bouillon
1/4 cup chopped green pepper
1/2 teaspoon salt
1/4 teaspoon thyme

1 cup boiling water
1/2 cup chopped onion
1 16-ounce can tomatoes
dash pepper

If using canned salmon, drain, remove skin and bones, and break up into chunks. Dissolve bouillon in boiling water. In a small skillet, melt butter and cook onion and green pepper until tender; use low heat. Combine all ingredients. Cook for approximately 15 minutes to blend flavours. Serves 4 to 6.

PORT DOVER CHINOOK CAKES

4 cups cooked flaked chinook   1 cup cooked rice
1 cup milk   2 eggs, beaten
1 1/2 cups bread crumbs   2 onions, chopped
1/2 cup chopped celery   1 teaspoon salt
1 cup drained and crushed pineapple
2 teaspoons worcestershire sauce

Form all ingredients into patties. Fry in skillet with hot oil.

BAKED STUFFED GEORGIAN BAY CHINOOK

After cleaning, leave head and tail on fish. Clean and wash fish well. Salt interior and then stuff with a highly seasoned bread stuffing, a shellfish stuffing or thinly sliced vegetables, together with herbs and butter. If backbone is removed, allow one cup of stuffing per pound of fish; otherwise, 3/4 cup per pound. Close the opening of the fish with small skewers and lace with string.

Place on buttered baking sheet or on a bed of finely cut leeks, carrots, onions and celery. Oil the fish well and add a cup or two of white wine (bake at 450°F). Allow 10 minutes per inch of thickness. Baste with a butter or oil, fresh lemon or wine.

Serve with a wine sauce made with pan juices, with tomato sauce made from pan juices, mushroom sauce or with lemon butter.

GORE BAY CHOWDER WITH MILK

3 pounds salmon
1 bay leaf
3 peppercorns
3 large potatoes, diced
2 large onions, sliced
salt to taste

water enough to cover fish
1 sprig parsley
1/4 teaspoon salt
1/4 pound salt pork, diced
6 cups milk
pepper to taste

Carefully place salmon in deep pot; cover with water (no more than that amount); add bay leaf, parsley, peppercorns, and salt; boil 15 minutes, or until salmon can be flaked with fork and broth is cooked down. While salmon is cooking, boil potatoes and prepare pork and onions as follows: place pork in skillet; fry over medium flame 15 minutes, or until golden brown and well done; add onions, brown 5 minutes, stirring constantly. Remove cooked salmon and flake in large pieces.

Heat deep soup tureen by letting it stand in very hot water. Place salmon, potatoes, onions, and salt pork in heated tureen; cover to keep hot. In a separate pot, heat milk to almost the boiling point; pour milk over hot ingredients; add salt and pepper. Serve piping hot in preheated chowder bowls. Serves 6 to 8.

SAVORY POACHED KING SALMON

4 salmon steaks, 6 ounces each
1 carrot, sliced
1 celery stalk, chopped
1/2 teaspoon thyme
pinch salt

1/2 onion, thinly sliced
2 cups water
10 peppercorns
juice of 1 lemon

Place cleaned salmon steaks in skillet and add remaining ingredients; liquid should barely cover fish. Simmer covered for 20 minutes. Using slotted spatula, transfer salmon to platter and serve hot. Serves 4.

OWEN SOUND BAY SALMON STEAKS

3 salmon steaks, 6 ounces each
1/3 cup butter, melted
1 teaspoon salt
1/4 teaspoon pepper
1 clove garlic
1 tablespoon onion, finely chopped

1/2 cup dry vermouth
1/8 cup lemon juice
1/4 teaspoon marjoram
1/4 teaspoon thyme
pinch sage

Place salmon steaks in a single layer in a shallow pan. Combine all other ingredients. Pour sauce over salmon and allow to marinate for 4 hours; turn steaks occasionally. Remove steaks, saving the sauce. Place steaks in a wire grill or basket or place them on grill 4 inches from hot coals for 8 minutes. Turn and cook other side, basting with sauce while steaks are cooking. Serves 3.

KINCARDINE SALMON STEAK DELIGHT

5 salmon steaks, 6 ounces each
1/4 cup parsley
2 tablespoons onion, grated
1/4 teaspoon salt

1/2 cup salad oil
1/4 cup lemon juice
1/2 teaspoon dry mustard
dash pepper

Place salmon in a shallow dish. Combine all other ingredients; pour over fish. Let stand at room temperature 2 hours, turning occasionally (or marinate in refrigerator 4 to 6 hours). Place salmon in well-greased wire broiler basket or on flat rack. Grill over medium-hot coals until lightly browned (6 to 8 minutes); baste with marinade and turn. Brush again with marinade; grill until fish flakes easily when tested with a fork (6 to 8 minutes longer). Serves 6.

COHO SALMON

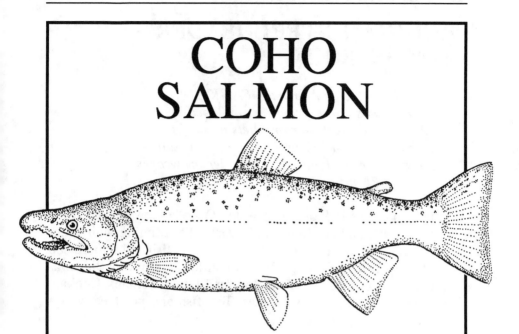

Native to the Pacific Northwest, the coho was introduced into the Great Lakes by the State of Michigan in the early 1960s. The coho or silver salmon is prized both for its pugnacious fighting ability, and its table value.

BAKED STUFFED SALMON DRESSING

4 tablespoons chopped onion　　*1 cup celery*
1/2 cup melted butter　　*1 1/2 teaspoons salt*
1/2 teaspoon lemon pepper　　*1 teaspoon sage*
3/4 teaspoon thyme　　*5 cups dry bread cubes*

Brown onions and celery in butter for 15 minutes. Add cooked vegetables and seasoning to bread cubes and mix thoroughly. If dressing appears dry add 4 tablespoons of milk.

MICHIGAN STEELHEADER'S SALMON BOIL

1 12 quart "Leyse Aluminum Fish Kettle"
15 medium sized potatoes, ends clipped
12 pounds of fresh salmon fillets or steaks
10 medium sized onions   2 cups salt
2 cups of drawn butter   lemon wedges
pepper to taste   parsley

Heat potatoes in 8 quarts of water. Once boiling begins, add 1 cup of salt and also onions if desired. Start timing with water boiling. Boil potatoes for 20 minutes. Add fish and 1 more cup of salt—fish is placed in basket and lowered into boiling water, salt is poured over fish. Boil for 12 more minutes. Cooking time may vary 2 or 3 minutes. Test fish and potatoes with a fork, drain and serve.

Potatoes, fish and onions are best served with drawn butter and parsley. Little if any salt is absorbed into the fish.

Ontario anglers have been missing the boat on this tasty recipe. Our Michigan counterparts are attracted to a fish boil by the hundreds when the salmon and trout are hitting. Leyse Aluminum Fish Kettles are available in four sizes and can be obtained from Acklands Ltd., Consumer Products Division, 1325 Lawrence Ave. E., Toronto.

Any soft-finned fish can be cooked with this salmon boil technique.

BAKED STUFFED PORT CREDIT COHO SALMON

7 to 10 pound Lake Ontario coho salmon
2 teaspoons salt
bread stuffing (recipe below)
6 slices of bacon

Wash and dry salmon. Sprinkle inside and out with salt. Stuff inside of coho loosely and sew closed with string or skewers. Lay coho in well greased baking pan. Position bacon slices over fish and bake at 350°F for 1 hour. Occasionally baste with drippings or melted fat. Serve immediately with white wine, with or without sauce.

COHO OVER THE COALS

1/2 cup barbecue sauce   *3/4 cup butter*
juice of 2 lemons   *6 to 8 pound coho salmon*
1 tablespoon worcestershire sauce

Combine the first four ingredients and heat until butter just begins to bubble. Clean coho, remove scales and split along backbone to remove backbone as in filleting. Leave skin on the fish. Position fish on well greased rack and place another well greased rack of the same size on top of the salmon. Place on hot barbecue grill 2 to 3 inches above coals and cook for 10 to 15 minutes with flesh side down. Turn rack over with skin side down and begin basting with sauce. Do not overcook. Done in 25 minutes.

PORT DALHOUSIE COHO BARBECUE

4 to 8 ounce coho steaks   *juice of 1 lemon*
2 tablespoons vegetable oil   *2 tablespoons sesame seeds*
1 1/2 tablespoons brown sugar   *1/2 teaspoon oregano*
1 teaspoon worcestershire sauce *1/4 teaspoon dry mustard*
1 tablespoon finely chopped parsle
1-8 ounce can tomato cheese sauce

Baste salmon steaks with oil and sprinkle with sesame seeds. Combine everything else but parsley in a saucepan and simmer gently for 12 minutes. Place steaks on a hot grill 2 to 3 inches from hot coals. Baste frequently with sauce. Cook about 7 minutes and then carefully turn steaks and cook other sides. Brown and add parsley to remaining sauce and serve with salmon.

COHO SPREAD

1 smoked coho, ground
1/4 teaspoon garlic powder
2 8-ounce packages cream cheese
1 small jar horseradish sauce
1 tablespoon chopped onion
1 small jar limburger cheese spread
1 teaspoon Worcestershire sauce
1 large chopped green pepper
1 tablespoon chopped pimento

Leave all items to warm at room temperature. Mix all items together. Add enough mayonnaise so that mix is spreadable. Serve on crackers or rye bread.

SUPERIOR SALMON AND PEAS

1 cup cooked left-over flaked salmon
1 1/2 pint drained peas   *1/8 teaspoon pepper*
3 tablespoons flour   *4 tablespoons butter*
1 cup milk   *1/2 teaspoon salt*
toast

Melt butter and add in flour, seasoning and milk. Cook till thick. Add and blend peas and salmon. Serve on toast.

BRONTE COHO AND WINE

4 to 6 ounce salmon steaks   *1/2 teaspoon onion powder*
3/4 cup Rosé wine   *1/4 teaspoon pepper*
1/4 teaspoon marjoram   *seasoning salt to taste*

Place coho in shallow pan. Stir together wine, marjoram, onion powder and pepper. Pour over steaks. Place in refrigerator for 6 hours, turning steaks once or twice. Drain well. Grill fish until steak flakes easily with a fork. Turn once during cooking and season with salt.

GREAT LAKES COHO SALMON STUFFED EGGS

1/2 cup of canned coho salmon   *12 hard boiled eggs*
1 anchovy fillet   *1/4 cup of butter*
1 teaspoon worcestershire sauce *salt and pepper*

Cut eggs in halves lengthwise. Take out yolks. Rub salmon, anchovy and egg yolks through a sieve, or whirl in a blender. Cream butter and add salmon mixture, worcestershire sauce and seasoning to taste. Stuff egg whites with mixture.

DONNA GEBERDT'S FAMOUS SALMON COOK-OUT

4 pounds salmon fillets   *1/2 cup French Dressing*
2 tablespoons lemon juice   *3 tablespoons grated onion*
2 teaspoons salt   *pepper and garlic to taste*

Cut fillets into serving size portions. Place in a well greased hinged wire grill. Mix remaining ingredients in a bowl. Baste fish with sauce and barbecue approximately 5 inches away from moderately hot coals for 8 minutes. Baste with sauce frequently. Turn and cook fillets until fish flakes easily. This cook-out serves upwards of 10 hungry anglers.

OUR FAVOURITE – SALMON FILLETS IN FOIL

4 pounds salmon fillets   *4 teaspoons salt*
1/4 teaspoons pepper   *1/4 cup butter, melted*
3 tablespoons chopped parsley   *3 tablespoons lemon juice*
1/2 teaspoon dill seed   *10 thin slices of onion*
3 cups of sliced green peppers   *6 slices Swiss cheese*
6 large squares of aluminum foil—doubled

Cut fillets in to 6 serving portions and sprinkle with salt and pepper to taste. Combine parsley, lemon juice, salt, dill seed. Melt butter. Place 1 teaspoon of butter and mixture on one half of each double square of foil and place fish over it. Separate onion into rings and place on fish. top each onion with 1/2 cup of green peppers. Divided remaining butter over green peppers. Cover with cheese slices. Fold foil over cheese and seal edges with double folds. Place packages directly on hot coals. Allow 10 to 12 minutes cooking time.

SIMPLE SALMON TOSSER

1 15 1/2-ounce can salmon   dash salt
2 tablespoons lemon juice   dash cayenne
1/2 cup mayonnaise   2/3 cup celery, diced
1 teaspoon prepared horseradish 1/4 cup stuffed olives, sliced
2 tablespoons chives, chopped   lettuce to garnish
2 eggs, hard-cooked & chopped   paprika to garnish

Drain salmon, remove skin and bones, and flake; sprinkle with lemon juice. In a large mixing bowl blend mayonnaise and horseradish; add salt and cayenne. Mix celery, olives, 1 table-spoon chives, and eggs with mayonnaise mixture; add salmon carefully. Serve on crisp lettuce leaves on a prechilled salad plate. Sprinkle with paprika and remaining chopped chives. Serves 4 to 6.

COLPOY BAY SALMON BARBECUE

4 pan-sized salmon   salt to taste
1/2 cup catsup   1/4 cup water
1/4 cup lemon juice   1/8 cup molasses
1/2 teaspoon dry mustard   1/4 cup butter
1 small onion, minced   1 tablespoon soy sauce

Scale salmon and remove back and belly fins leaving heads and tails on; wash and salt inside of cavities. Prepare charcoal or pit fire. Oil grill. Mix all remaining ingredients for sauce in pan on fire. Allow sauce to simmer for 10 minutes.

When fire is ready, place grill over fire. Oil fish and baste with sauce. Fish should be about 6 to 8 inches from heat; let fish broil about 5 minutes to a side, basting often; fish is cooked when flesh in centre is no longer transparent. Just before serving, brush a final coating of sauce over fish. Serves 4.

SALMON NOODLES SPECTACULAR

1 15 1/2-ounce can salmon
1 8-ounce package medium-sized noodles
2 tablespoons butter or margarine, melted
1/4 cup butter or margarine, melted
2 tablespoons flour   *1 cup milk*
dash Tabasco   *salt to taste*
1 cup fresh bread crumbs *pepper to taste*

Preheat oven to 350°F. Drain and flake salmon; remove skin and bones. Cook noodles according to package directions; drain well and rinse. Grease a 2-quart casserole. In saucepan melt 2 tablespoons of butter; stir in flour. Gradually stir in milk and cook, stirring until sauce is smooth and thickened. Stir in salmon, Tabasco, salt and pepper. Arrange alternate layers of salmon, sauce and noodles in casserole, finishing with sauce. In a small bowl mix crumbs with butter; sprinkle over mixture in casserole. Bake for 30 minutes. Serves 6.

SALMON A LA KING

1 15 1/2-ounce can salmon   1/2 cup butter, melted
1/2 cup celery, chopped   1/2 green pepper, chopped
1/4 cup flour   1/2 teaspoon salt
1 1/2 cups salmon liquid and milk, combined
1 cup mushrooms, cooked and sliced
2 tablespoons chopped pimento
patty shell, toast or cooked rice

Drain salmon, reserving liquid; remove skin and bones and break into small chunks. Melt butter in a pan; add celery and green pepper; cook over low heat until vegetables are tender. Gradually add flour and salt; stir until smooth. Slowly add salmon liquid and milk; cook gently, stirring until sauce is thick and smooth. Add salmon, mushrooms, and pimento. Heat mixture and serve in a patty shell. Serves 6.

FISHERMAN'S OMELET

one 7 3/4-ounce can salmon   6 eggs, separated
1 tablespoon parsley, chopped   1 teaspoon chives, chopped
1/2 teaspoon salt   dash oregano
2 tablespoons butter, melted   dash pepper
1/3 cup salmon liquid and water, combined

Preheat oven to 350°. Drain and remove skin and bones from salmon, reserving liquid; flake salmon. Beat egg whites until stiff; set aside. Beat egg yolks until thick and lemon coloured; add next 6 ingredients. Add salmon and mix well. Fold into egg white mixture. Pour omelet mixture into hot, buttered 10-inch fry pan and spread evenly. Cook over low heat for 3 to 5 minutes or until lightly browned on bottom. Bake for 2 to 5 minutes or until a knife inserted in the centre comes out clean. Cut part way through centre of omelet and fold in half. Serve immediately on a warm platter. Serves 6.

SMALLMOUTH BASS

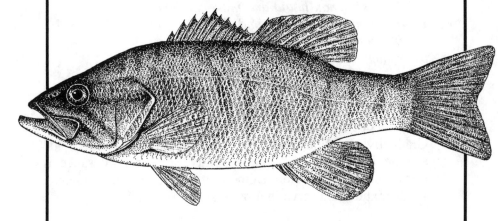

Pound for pound, this member of the sunfish family is often regarded as North America's fightingest freshwater game fish. Noted for its bad attitude and surface-breaking leaps the smallmouth bass readily attacks live bait, spinners, spoons and plugs.

PORT DOVER CORN MEAL SMALLMOUTH

6 smallmouth bass fillets
6 pieces of cooked bacon strips
1/2 cup flour
3/4 cup corn meal
2 eggs
1/4 cup milk

Mix flour and corn meal together. Dip fillets in egg and milk mix. Dip bass fillets in flour and corn meal mix. Fry fillets in hot bacon fat until flaky.

MIKE'S BEER BATTER SMALLMOUTH

3 pounds smallmouth fillets   *2 cups beer*
2 cups pancake flour   *2 eggs*
seasoning of salt, pepper and garlic salt

Mix pancake flour with beer. Add 2 slightly beaten eggs and seasoning. Mix thoroughly. Immerse fillets in mixture and drain off excess. Deep fry until golden. Drain off oil and serve with cold beer.

TO AVOID ANY FISHY TASTE:
We suggest filleting the fish or scaling the bass and freezing the scaled bass for a day or two.

MOHAWK BAY BASS SUPREME

2 pounds of Lake Erie smallmouth fillets
2 lemons   *6 tablespoons butter*
seasoned flour   *1 dash worcestershire sauce*
(salt, pepper, onion salt)   *1 dash soy sauce*
1 cup sherry   *1 finely chopped onion*
1 tablespoon chopped parsley

Chill smallmouth fillets with juice of two lemons. Cover fillets with flour. Sauté finely chopped onion in butter. Add fillets and sauté bass until golden brown. Remove bass from pan. Add 4 tablespoons of sherry to drippings in pan. Add remaining sherry, worcestershire sauce, parsley and soy sauce and stir until heated. Bass is served with sauce spread evenly on top. Parsley sprigs and lemon slices are used to garnish fillets.

GOLDEN SMALLMOUTH FISH PUFFS

1 pound flaked smallmouth bass
4 well beaten eggs   4 stiffly beaten egg whites
4 teaspoons paprika   3/4 teaspoon salt
1 3/4 cups mashed potatoes   pepper to taste

Preheat deep fryer to 340°F. Mix together all ingredients except egg whites. Fold in beaten whites. Measure portions by teaspoon size. Lower portions into hot oil. Cook just under 5 minutes or until golden brown. Drain and serve hot with sliced lemon and tartar sauce.

GANANOQUE BASS AND TOMATO BAKE

6 to 8 medium-sized small mouth fillets
3 tablespoons butter   2 small chopped onions
2 to 3 tomatoes, peeled & sliced   1 bay leaf
3 tablespoons oil   1 1/2 teaspoons thyme
1 1/2 teaspoons salt   1/2 cup fine bread crumbs
1 teaspoon pepper

Sauté onions, seasonings and tomatoes in oil. Arrange fish in baking dish and pour sauce over. Oven bake for 25 to 30 minutes at 375°F. Sprinkle bread crumbs over everything and broil for 2 to 3 minutes until golden brown.

BROILED BARBECUE BLACK BASS

2 pounds fresh smallmouth fillets
1/2 cup melted butter   *1/4 cup tomato catsup*
2 tablespoons minced onions   *1 teaspoon salt*
2 tablespoons lemon juice   *parsley*
1 teaspoon worcestershire sauce

Place fillets on greased broiler pan. Mix butter, lemon juice, ketchup, worcestershire, salt and onion. Heat mixture and pour over fillets. Place 2 to 4 inches from under broiler and broil one side only for 10 minutes. Ready when fish flakes. Garnish with parsley.

THERESA'S PINEAPPLE SMALLMOUTH BASS FILLETS

6 smallmouth bass fillets   *1 tablespoon lime juice*
3/4 cup pineapple juice   *salt, pepper to taste*
3 teaspoons worcestershire sauce

Place bass fillets in shallow dish. Combine other ingredients and pour over perch. Marinate fish in refrigerator 1 1/2 hours. Turn once. Drain, reserving marinade. Place bass on greased rack of broiler pan. Broil 4 inches from heat for 10 minutes or until fish flakes easily. Brush occasionally with marinade. Warm remaining marinade and spoon over fish.

KINGSTON SMALLMOUTH FISH PATTIES

2 1/2 pounds of cooked smallmouth bass fillets
1/2 onion (chopped)   *salt and pepper to taste*
small green pepper   *1/2 cup waffle mix*
1/2 cup milk   *garlic to taste*
1 egg

Flake smallmouth fillets. Mix eggs, smallmouth and all other ingredients thoroughly. Prepare desired size patties from mixture. Cook smallmouth patties in 1/4 inch of hot vegetable oil on both sides until golden.

LONG POINT BAY BUTTERMILK SMALLMOUTH

3 pounds of Lake Erie smallmouth bass fillets
1 1/4 cups of biscuit mix   *Mazola oil*
1 1/4 cups of buttermilk   *salt, pepper, garlic to taste*

Lay fillets in buttermilk for one hour. Shake off excess buttermilk. Sprinkle with spices. Cover in biscuit mix. Deep fry briefly in hot oil until fillets are golden brown.

BRONTE CREEK BASS PANCAKES

1 cup of cooked smallmouth flakes
1 cup flour   *2 eggs, well beaten*
1/2 teaspoon salt   *1/2 cup milk*
1/2 teaspoon baking powder   *chopped onion*

Mix ingredients. Fry as for any pancakes. Add more milk if batter is too thick.

THOUSAND ISLAND BAKED BARBECUED SMALLMOUTH

2 pounds of bass fillets
4 teaspoons instant minced onions
1 teaspoon prepared mustard
6 tablespoons of bottled seafood cocktail sauce

2 teaspoons lemon juice
6 tablespoons water
1/2 teaspoon salt

Mix all ingredients except fish in bowl. Preheat oven to 450°F. Place smallmouth in shallow baking dish. Cover with sauce. Bake 20 minutes or until flaky.

DESERONTO BRONZEBACK STEW

3 pounds of cubed fillets of bass
salad oil
1 diced clove garlic
1 diced medium onion
1 quart water
2 sweet basil leaves
1 bay leaf
parsley flakes

1 diced carrot
1 stalk diced celery
1 cup tomato puree
3 diced potatoes
2 cups chopped cabbage
dash worcestershire sauce
1 teaspoon sugar

Cover bottom of 4 quart pot with cooking oil. When oil is hot add cubed fish fillets. As you stir, break fish as they cook. Add garlic and onion for approximately 2 minutes. Add 2 cups water, bay leaf, sweet basil, and parsley flakes. Allow to simmer for 10 minutes. Add celery and carrots and continue to simmer for 30 minutes. Use all remaining items, but only enough water to give a stew-like texture. Continue to simmer until vegetables are soft and tender. Add salt and pepper to taste.

GRAVELLY BAY POACHED SMALLMOUTH WITH EGG SAUCE

2 pounds smallmouth fillets	2 sprigs of parsley
2 cups boiling water	1 bay leaf
1/4 cup lemon juice	paprika
1 thinly sliced onion	egg sauce
3 peppercorn	1 teaspoon salt

Place smallmouth fillets in a greased 10 inch fry pan. Add remaining ingredients. Cover and simmer until fish flakes (approximately 10 minutes). Carefully remove fillets to a hot platter. Pour egg sauce over fish. Sprinkle with paprika.

EGG SAUCE:

1/4 cup of butter	1 1/4 cup milk
2 tablespoons of flour	1/2 teaspoons salt
3/4 teaspoons powdered mustard	dash pepper
1 tablespoon chopped parsley	2 chopped hard boiled eggs

Melt butter. Stir in flour and seasonings. At the same time add milk. Cook until thick and smooth. Stirring continuously add eggs and parsley.

WELLINGTON BEACH BAKED SMALLMOUTH

2 pounds smallmouth fillets	3/4 teaspoons salt
3 tablespoons chopped onion	1 cup grated cheese
1 can Campbell's Cream of Tomato Soup	

Slice fillets into desired servings. Place fillets into a well greased baking dish. Stir up soup, pepper, salt and onions. Pour over fish fillets. Top evenly with grated cheese. Bake in oven at 350°F for 30 minutes.

LARGEMOUTH BASS

The bucketmouth enters the sport fishery at less than half a pound and can weigh 20 pounds or more. While catch-and-release fishing is popular, anglers still pursue the largemouth for its table qualities. The flesh of the largemouth bass is white, flaky and low in oil. Originally, the largemouth was found in southeastern Canada, through the Great Lakes and south in the Mississippi Valley to Mexico and Florida. Stocking programs have delivered the bass to just about every state. The largemouth is our top game fish.

BUCKETMOUTH ITALIAN STYLE

3 pounds largemouth fillets   *1 1/4 cups flour*
4 eggs   *4 tablespoons flat beer*
3 tablespoons grated parmesan cheese

Beat eggs well, adding cheese, flour and salt, stirring continuously. Continue to stir and add beer. Roll fillets in flour, then dip in batter, allowing excess batter to fall from fillets. Carefully lower fillets into hot oil and cook for 2 to 3 minutes or until golden brown in color.

KAWARTHA DEEP FRIED LARGEMOUTH

3 pounds largemouth bass fillets   2 cups of self-rising flour
2 bottles of ale   2 eggs
1/2 teaspoon baking soda   salt and pepper to season

Cut bass fillets into finger sizes 3 to 4 inches long, and dry on paper towel. Season with salt and pepper. Mix eggs, beer, baking soda, flour, salt and pepper together. Stir until mix is not too thin or not too thick. Immerse fillets, thoroughly covering. Carefully lower fillets into hot (375°F) oil. Care should be taken that fillets do not stick to bottom of deep fryer. Continue cooking for approximately 5 to 6 minutes or until golden brown. Serve with beer and tartar sauce.

LARGEMOUTH ITALIAN STYLE

3 pounds largemouth fillets   garlic to taste
6 tablespoons snipped parsley   1/4 teaspoon pepper
1/2 teaspoon dried oregano leaves
2 16 ounce jars of Bravo spaghetti sauce
2 cups shredded mozzarella cheese

Preheat oven to 350°F. Place bass fillets in large greased baking dish. Cover fillets with spaghetti sauce. Sprinkle with oregano, parsley, and pepper. Cover with mozzarella. Bake for 20 to 30 minutes until bass flakes easily with fork.

LARGEMOUTH AMANDINE

2 pounds fresh bass fillets　　*1/4 pound butter*
1/2 cup white wine　　*almond slivers*

Melt butter in shallow baking dish until it is a deep golden brown. Season fillets with salt and pepper to taste. Dip both sides of fillets in butter and position in baking dish. Boil wine and then pour over fillets. Bake fillets at 350°F for approximately 25 minutes or until flaky. Before serving, sprinkle fillets with almond slivers.

BUCKHORN LAKE LARGEMOUTH SCRAMBLE

1 cup cooked flaked largemouth　*3 to 5 eggs*
1/4 cup milk　　*2 tablespoons butter*
salt and pepper to taste　　*chopped onions*

Take eggs and mix with largemouth flakes. Add milk. Fry in melted butter. This meal is quick, delicious and also solves the problem of what to do with leftover fish.

BASS PUFFS

1 cup cooked flaked largemouth　*1 cup mashed potatoes*
1/2 cup milk　　*2 eggs*
1/2 teaspoon paprika　　*salt and pepper to taste*

Stir flaked bass, milk, salt, pepper, paprika and one egg in mixing bowl. Place in greased casserole dish and bake for 20 minutes at 350°F. Beat remaining egg white until stiff. Stir in yolk and spread mixture over bass. Brown topping. Serves 4.

BAKED BUCKETMOUTH AND POTATOES

2 pounds of largemouth fillets   *3 tablespoons butter*
1 1/3 pounds potatoes (peeled and thinly sliced)
1 cup chopped onions   *1/2 teaspoons pepper*
2 teaspoons salt   *2 cups milk*
3 tablespoons dry bread crumbs 2 eggs

Cut largemouth into bite-sized pieces. Saute onion bits in hot buttered frying pan for 5 to 10 minutes. Pre-grease a 2 quart baking dish. Stack successive layers of potatoes, bass and onions. Sprinkle each layer with salt and pepper. Finish your layer with potatoes and cover with bread crumbs. Scramble eggs and milk until frothy. Pour over potatoes in baking dish. Place in pre-heated 350°F oven for 1 hour.

BUCKHORN BAKED STUFFED BASS ROLLS

2 pounds of bass fillets   *1/2 cup flour*
2 tablespoons lemon juice   *1 teaspoon salt*
favourite bread stuffing recipe dash of pepper

Sprinkle fillets with salt, pepper and lemon juice. Place a ball of stuffing on each fillet, roll and tie securely with string. Roll in flour and brown in hot fat. Place rolls in a well greased, covered casserole dish and bake in moderate oven, 350°F for 30 minutes or until fish flakes with fork. Remove string, garnish and serve hot.

NAPANEE STUFFED TOMATO LARGEMOUTH

3 pounds largemouth bass　　*1/4 cup cold water*
2 cups bread crumbs　　*1/4 cup melted butter*
2 tablespoons chopped parsley　*1/2 teaspoon salt*
Napanee Tomato Sauce

Clean and scale largemouth. Wipe cavity and then rub with salt. Combine all ingredients except special tomato sauce to make dressing. Fill the cavity of the largemouth with the dressing and sew closed. Baste the outside of bass with melted butter. Pour tomato sauce over fish. Bake in pre-heated 375°F oven for 35 to 45 minutes.

NAPANEE TOMATO SAUCE

2 cups of canned tomatoes　　*1 bay leaf*
1 1/2 stalks of chopped celery　*1 teaspoon salt*
3 tablespoons green pepper　　*3 tablespoons onion*

Combine all ingredients, and cook over medium heat for 10 minutes. Cover over fish and bake for required time.

LAKE ERIE LARGEMOUTH AND ALE DEEP-FRY

3 pounds small fillets　　*2 cups of ale*
3 cups of pancake mix　　*3 eggs*
1 teaspoon pepper　　　*1 1/2 teaspoons salt*
garlic to taste

Mix pancake flour, ale, garlic, salt and pepper. Beat egg and add to mix to make a smooth batter. Lower bass into batter and then shake off excess batter. Fry fillets in hot oil until light brown. Serve with tartar sauce or lemon slices.

GEORGIAN BAY LARGEMOUTH AND MUSHROOM

6 medium sized bass fillets
1/2 teaspoon salt
4 tablespoons white wine
lemon wedges
1 4 ounce can of sliced mushrooms

2/3 cup heavy cream
1/2 teaspoon pepper
3 tablespoons cornstarch

Blend cream, cornstarch, mushrooms, salt and pepper into smooth sauce. Place bass fillets in greased baking pan. Cover bass with sauce. Place pan in pre-heated 350°F oven. Bake for 15 to 20 minutes.

STONEY LAKE BROILED LARGEMOUTH FILLETS

6 good sized fillets
3 tablespoons of soy sauce
6 tablespoons of salad dressing

2 sliced lemons
salt and pepper to taste
garlic to taste

Mix salad dressing, garlic, soy sauce. Cover all sides of fillets with sauce mixture. Allow fillets to sit for 1 hour. Broil bass for 6 to 8 minutes 5 inches from source of heat. Flip fillets and wipe any remaining sauce on fish. Cook for another 4 to 5 minutes.

HUNGRY MAN'S BASS PATTIES AND BEANS

3 cups of flaked fillets
1 1/2 cups of cracker crumbs
1/3 cup of diced onions
1 large can of baked beans

3 eggs
1/3 cup of water
salt and pepper to taste

Beat eggs. Combine eggs with all ingredients except beans. Form fish patties that are easy to manage and about 1/2 inch thick. Fry patties in hot oil much as in the same manner as you would hamburger. Heat up the beans and share your plates with bass patties and beans.

TRENT RIVER LARGEMOUTH AND VEGGIES

2 pounds of fillets
1/3 cup chopped onion
1/2 cup chopped green pepper
1/3 cup butter
4 tablespoons white wine
1 1/2 tablespoons snipped parsley

3/4 cup chopped celery
1 large tomato
1/3 cup diced carrot
1/2 cup bread crumbs
salt and pepper to taste

In small frying pan cook and mix celery, green pepper, onion, carrot and butter on medium heat until tender. Set aside on warm burner. Grease 9" X 13" baking dish. Peel and dice tomato and mix in a bowl with bread, salt, pepper, parsley and vegetables. Arrange fillets in greased dish. Cover with vegetable mix. Sprinkle with white wine and bake in preheated 350°F oven for 20 minutes. Check so that bass flakes easily.

CHANNEL CATFISH

'Old Whiskers' is often looked upon with disgust as a garbage-eater. But nothing could be farther from the truth. Fresh out of the Great Lakes, a clear lake or pond, or the mighty Mississippi, catfish and bullheads are now widespread across America and Canada. Because of their table quality, catfish bring a high price on the commercial market. These fish offer excellent angling opportunities for adults and youngsters alike.

SAUGEEN RIVER CHANNEL CAT

4 pounds catfish fillets   *salt and pepper to taste*
1/4 cup bacon drippings   *juice of one lemon*

Clean and wipe catfish fillets. Season with salt and pepper. Sauté in hot bacon drippings until browned on both sides. Drain on paper towel. Sprinkle with lemon juice.

FRENCH FRIED CHANNEL CATFISH

5 pounds catfish fillets
3 cups salted cornmeal
lemon juice

2 cans evaporated milk
salt to taste
melted butter

Skin and fillet fish. Cut crosswise into 1 inch fillets. Salt fillets and dip into evaporated milk. Roll in cornmeal.

Carefully lower into deep fryer and cook until golden brown. Fish fried in evaporated milk tends to burn easily so be sure to remove as soon as golden. Serve with lemon juice and melted butter.

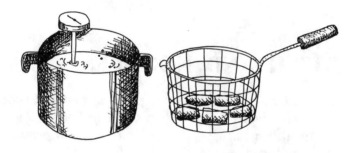

DUNNVILLE BAKED CATFISH

4 pounds catfish fillets
1/2 teaspoon dry mustard
1/2 teaspoon marjoram
3/4 cups flour

5 tablespoons butter
1/4 teaspoon tarragon
2 cans condensed milk

Melt butter in baking dish. Mix flour, mustard, marjoram and tarragon. Dip catfish in milk and then roll in flour mixture. Lay them in butter dish and bake for 20 minutes at 325°F. Remove from oven, turn and bake for another 15 minutes. Serve with cold beer and tartar sauce.

BILL AND THERESA'S COLPOY BAY CATFISH

5 good-sized catfish fillets
1/4 cup bacon fat
salt and pepper to taste
pinch of rosemary

1 cup cornmeal
1 cup canned milk
1/4 teaspoon thyme

Season fillets with salt and pepper. Dip fillets in milk then roll in cornmeal. Melt bacon fat in cast iron skillet and fry fish when fat is hot. Fish should be allowed to fry 3 to 5 minutes on each side. Season each side before turning with thyme and rosemary. Serve with lemon butter and hush puppies.

CATFISH AND NOODLES

6 catfish fillets (4 pounds)
1/4 pound butter
1 tablespoon salt
6 strips bacon

3 cups cooked noodles
1 cup flour
1 teaspoon pepper
6 olives

Combine flour, salt, pepper and fillets in a small plastic bag and shake well. Once fillets are completely covered remove and fry in hot butter until golden. Remove and towel dry. Position one strip of bacon and an olive on each fillet with toothpick. Bake in oven at 350°F for 15 minutes. Serve with noodles.

TERESA J's FAMOUS CATFISH FRY

2 pounds of catfish fillets
1/2 teaspoon ground thyme
1/2 teaspoon ground pepper
1/4 teaspoon lemon pepper

1 cup flour
1/2 teaspoon salt
1/2 teaspoon paprika

Combine all ingredients in a quart jar and shake well. Use two heaping tablespoons per fillet in a plastic bag and shake fillet until covered. Place bacon strips and chopped onion in a frying pan and simmer until both sides of bacon are crisp. Fry fish in bacon fat until golden brown.

SAUGEEN RIVER CATFISH GUMBO

2 pounds catfish fillets
1/2 cup finely chopped celery
1/2 cup finely chopped onion
1 pound of fresh tomatoes
2 teaspoons salt
1 teaspoon liquid hot pepper sauce
1 package frozen okra (10 ounce)
1/2 cup finely chopped green peppers
1 whole bay leaf

3 cups of boiling water
1/4 cup oil
1 garlic clove
2 beef bouillon cubes
1/4 teaspoon pepper

Cut fillets into one inch chunks. Combine green pepper, celery, garlic and onion and fry in oil until ingredients are tender. Add bouillon cubes to boiling water, okra, tomatoes, and the seasonings. Add liquid mixture to green pepper mix. Cover and simmer for 30 minutes. Add fish, cover and simmer until catfish flakes easily. Remove bay leaf. Great over wild rice.

FRENCH RIVER FRIED CATFISH

6 pounds of catfish fillets   *3 pieces of garlic*
1/2 pound butter   *peanut oil*
salt, pepper and garlic to taste   *ground corn meal*

Pour peanut oil 1/4 inch deep in frying pan. Add garlic and cook for 30 minutes. Discard garlic. Rub fish with butter and sprinkle with salt and pepper. Roll fish fillets in corn meal until covered thoroughly. Increase garlic butter temperature to medium high. Lay fillets in pan and fry until both sides are crispy, light brown.

FORT ERIE CATFISH SURPRISE

5 pounds of catfish fillets   *3 eggs*
2 cups of bread crumbs   *1 teaspoon black pepper*
1 teaspoon seafood seasoning   *1 tablespoon sea salt*
pinch of garlic   *pinch of onion salt*
1 pinch red pepper

Beat eggs and dip fillets in egg. Place all dry ingredients in a plastic bag and shake to mix. Shake excess egg off fillets and place fillets one at a time in bag and mix until coated. Arrange fillets on a greased baking rack. Bake for 45 minutes at 350 degrees. Best served with lemon tea and lemon wedges.

SMOKED CATFISH IN TOMATOES

2 pounds smoked catfish fillets   *1/4 teaspoon pepper*
1 can (19 ounces) tomatoes   *1 medium sliced onion*
1/2 teaspoon oregano

Place catfish in baking dish. Combine remaining ingredients in a saucepan and simmer for 10 minutes. Pour sauce over fish and bake in a hot oven at 450 degrees until fish flakes easily when tested with a fork.

FRIED CATFISH WITH SPANISH SAUCE

3 pounds catfish fillets   *1/2 can of tomato sauce*
6 chopped cloves of garlic   *2 tablespoons melted butter*
1/2 cup finely chopped onions

Fry onion and garlic in butter until tender. Add tomato and cook 5 minutes longer. Roll catfish in flour and brown on both sides in butter. Pour sauce over fish, cover and cook slowly for 10 more minutes.

PANFISH

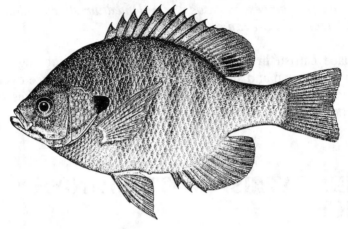

Children from 4 to 84 all love panfish. Whether it be the crappie, silver bass or sunfish, panfish are easy to catch and delicious to eat. Small hooks and small baits (grubs, worms, spinners and jigs) can account for a pail full of 4- to 10-inch panfish. These tasty critters are found from the Pacific to the Atlantic and are loved by all.

OLD SOUTH FANCY SUNFISH FILLETS

3 pounds sunfish or crappie fillets
1 1/2 cups prepared pancake mix
1 1/2 cups of white wine   *1 1/2 teaspoons pepper*
1 1/2 teaspoons salt   *3/4 cup butter*

Salt and pepper fillets. Marinate fillets in wine for 1 1/2 hours. Roll fillets in pancake mix. Carefully lower fillets into skillet of hot butter and cook until golden in colour. Excellent with tartar sauce and french fries. Serves four people.

BAKED PANFISH AND MUSHROOMS

2 pounds panfish fillets
4 tablespoons butter
1/2 cup bread crumbs
2 tablespoons finely chopped onions
2 cans or 1 1/2 cups of fresh mushrooms chopped fine

1 teaspoon dill
1 teaspoon chives
parsley

Sauté onion, breadcrumbs and mushrooms in 4 tablespoons of butter for 10 minutes over low heat. Being careful not to burn mixture, add crumbs and butter as needed to make a spreadable consistency. With one minute remaining, add chives and dill. Salt and pepper fillets. Spread a thin layer of sautéed mixture in the bottom of a greased baking dish. Arrange fillets in a single layer in dish. Spread the remaining mixture over and around the fillets. Cover with thin layer of dried bread crumbs. Sprinkle lightly with melted butter, parsley and salt. Bake for 30 to 40 minutes at 325°F or until top is brown.

DEVILED BLUEGILL

4 cups of bluegill meat (drop fillets in boiling water, bring to a boil again—remove and drain).
1 cup milk
1 1/2 tablespoons grated onion
3 tablespoons chopped parsley
3/4 teaspoon salt
1 teaspoon dry mustard
1 cup of crumbled corn flakes
3 tablespoons worcestershire sauce
4 thick slice of white bread, crusts removed

1/4 pound butter
dash of pepper
1 green pepper
dash Tabasco sauce
1 finely cut pimento

Cook everything but the fish for 10 minutes over medium heat, stirring. Then add the fish and cook five minutes. Place in a flat casserole and sprinkle crumbled corn flakes over the top. Brown in a 350°F oven for 15 minutes. Serves six people.

GEORGIAN BAY CRAPPIE AND BEER RECIPE

2 pounds filleted and skinned crappie
2 cups pancake flour   *1 1/2 cups beer*
2 eggs   *1 teaspoon salt*
1/2 teaspoon pepper

Beat egg. Combine with beer, pancake flour, salt and pepper, mixing into a smooth batter. Dip fillets into batter, draining off excess. Carefully lower fillets into hot (375°F) oil. Cook for no more than 2 minutes. Drain and eat 'em while they're hot!

UPPER NIAGARA CRUNCHY CRAPPIE

1 1/2 pounds of crappie fillets   *1 cup evaporated milk*
1 egg   *1/8 teaspoon salt*
1/8 teaspoon pepper   *2 cups cracker crumbs*
4 tablespoons vegetable oil

Use a shallow dish to blend egg and milk. On a plate mix cracker crumbs, salt and pepper. Dip crappie fillets in milk and then coat with cracker crumbs. Heat oil in small frying pan. Fry crappie three or four fillets at a time, for 2 or 3 minutes to a side. Once golden brown, drain on paper towel and serve with tartar sauce or sliced lemons.

ORANGE BUTTER SPECIAL

4 pounds fresh crappie fillets 2 teaspoons salt
4 teaspoons grated orange rind pepper seasoning to taste
4 teaspoons orange juice 6 tablespoons bacon fat

Spread crappie fillets evenly over a greased pan. Mix other ingredients and pour over fish. Bake at 450°F for 15 minutes or until fillets flake. Serves a crowd of 6 to 8 people.

RONDEAU BAY BLACK CRAPPIE DEEP FRY

4 pounds crappie fillets 2 cups of biscuit mix
2 cups of buttermilk salt, pepper, garlic to taste
bacon fat

Dip crappie fillets in buttermilk. Allow to swim for 20 minutes. Drain and season fillets with salt, pepper and garlic. Dip fish in biscuit flour. Deep fry in hot fat (375°F) until batter begins to golden.

LEMON FRIED SUNFISH

1 1/2 pound sunfish fillets 1 cup of flour
2 teaspoons grated lemon peel 1 cup of water
1/2 teaspoon salt 1/2 teaspoon pepper
vegetable oil

Combine flour, lemon peel, salt and pepper. Blend in cold water. Refrigerate for one hour. Pre-heat oil in deep fryer at 375°F. Coat fillets in flour and dip in cold batter. Fry three or four fillets at a time until golden brown. Drain and serve hot.

CHEESE TOPPED CRAPPIE FISHWICHES

1/2 pound cooked crappie fillets 1 egg white
1/4 cup Parmesan grated cheese 1/4 teaspoon onion salt
1 teaspoon dry mustard   hamburger buns
1/2 cup mayonnaise

Flake and mash crappie fillets. Beat egg white until stiff. Fold in Mayonnaise, cheese, onion, salt and mustard. Spread crappie fillets on hamburger buns. Spoon mix on top of flaked crappie. Place under broiler until puffy and golden brown.

WAUBAUSHENE BLACK CRAPPIE FISH CAKES

2 pounds flaked crappie   2 tablespoons mayonnaise
2 teaspoons seafood seasoning   1/2 teaspoon salt
2 tablespoons baking powder   1 teaspoon celery seed
2 eggs beaten   1 cup milk
2 slices bread in small pieces with crusts removed
2 teaspoons worcestershire sauce

Simmer crappie in salt water until flaky. Moisten bread with milk. Mix ingredients thoroughly. Shape into small cakes. Deep fry at 375°F until brown.

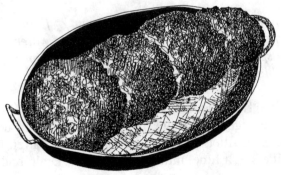

BELLE RIVER PANFISH DELIGHT

1 pound of panfish fillets
1 beaten egg
1/2 cup crushed crackers
1/8 teaspoon salt
1/8 teaspoon thyme

1/2 cup of flour
1/8 cup evaporated milk
1/8 teaspoon marjoram
1/8 teaspoon pepper

Mix flour, salt and pepper. Combine eggs and milk together. Now mix cracker crumbs together. Roll fillets in flour mix and then dip fillets into egg mix. Finally roll fillets into cracker crumb mixture. Carefully drop coated fillets into hot oil until golden brown.

PORT REYERSE PANFISH STIR-FRY

1 pound panfish fillets
2 tablespoons vegetable oil
1/2 cup of sliced green onion
1 pound fresh broccoli
1/4 cup teriyaki sauce
1/4 teaspoon garlic powder
1/4 cup vegetable oil

1 teaspoon corn starch
1 cup sliced carrot
1 cup sliced mushroom
1 tablespoon lemon juice
1/4 teaspoon salt
1/4 teaspoon pepper

Trim fillets into 1/4 inch diagonal strips. In a bowl toss fish strips with cornstarch until coated. Add two tablespoons of vegetable oil, teriyaki sauce, lemon juice, salt, pepper and garlic powder. Cover and refrigerate 30 minutes. Cut broccoli into flowerets, cut stems into thin slices. In small frying pan heat one quarter cup of vegetable oil. Add broccoli, green onion and carrot. Stir to coat all vegetables with oil. Cook and stir for 10 minutes over medium heat, until all vegetables are tender-crisp. Stir in panfish strips and marinade. Add mushrooms. Cook and stir over medium/high heat for 3 to 6 minutes. Fish should flake with fork.

BUBBLING PANFISH BAKE

3/4 pound of flaked panfish   *1/4 cup of chopped onion*
2 tablespoons butter   *1 cup of milk*
1 cup of shredded cheddar cheese
4 cups of cooked macaroni
2 tablespoons buttered bread crumbs
1 can condensed cream of mushroom soup

Cook onion in butter until tender. Add soup, milk, 3/4 cup of cheese. Fold in macaroni and fish . Pour into a 1 1/2 quart casserole. top with bread crumbs and remaining cheese. Bake in a 350°F oven for 35 minutes or until bubbling and lightly browned.

EASY BATTER FRIED PANFISH

1 pound panfish fillets   *vegetable oil*
1/4 teaspoon salt

Batter:
1 cup of flour   *2 teaspoons baking powder*
1/2 teaspoon salt   *1 egg*
1 cup milk

Heat oil in fryer to 375°F. Sprinkle fillets lightly with salt. For the batter mix together all dry ingredients. In a small bowl beat egg and stir in milk. Add the milk/egg mixture to the dry ingredients and beat only until smooth. Dip fish in batter and then into hot oil. Turn only once. Cook until fish is golden brown. Drain and serve with lemon.

WHITEFISH

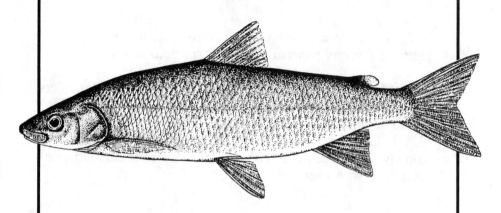

Seldom regarded for its fighting capabilities, the whitefish has no equal when properly prepared for the table. The soft mouth and light biting characteristics of the whitefish make this species difficult to catch. Found in the high mountain country of the Rockies, in the deep water of the Great Lakes and across Canada's far north, the whitefish is prized for its firm white flesh.

WAWA WHITEFISH IN THE OVEN

6 whitefish fillets
1/3 cup oil
1 1/2 teaspoons salt

1/2 cup cornmeal
1/2 cup milk
1/2 teaspoon pepper

Dip fillets in milk then in cornmeal, shaking off excess. Heat half the oil in a baking dish. Lay out fillets in dish and add the remaining oil over fish. Bake at 475°F for 20 minutes. Serve with lemon juice, tartar sauce, salt and pepper

TEMAGAMI WHITEFISH WITH SOUR CREAM AND MUSHROOMS

6 whitefish fillets
1 1/2 cups sliced mushrooms
salt, pepper and paprika to taste

1/2 cup butter
1 can mushroom soup
1 cup sour cream

Place fish fillets in a large buttered baking dish. Dot fillets with butter and sprinkle with salt, pepper and paprika. Sprinkle mushrooms over fillets. Bake for 15 minutes at 350°F. Combine sour cream and soup and heat until bubbling. Slowly pour sauce over fish and bake an additional 15 minutes. Top with sour cream and serve.

DEEPWATER WHITEFISH BALLS

5 pounds of dressed whitefish
1 carrot
2 teaspoons salt

1 onion
2 beaten eggs
1/4 teaspoon pepper

Wash fillets and skin fish. Place heads, tails, bones and skin in a large kettle. Put fillets, onion and carrot through food chopper. Add eggs, salt and pepper and mix well. Shape into balls 1 1/2 inches in diameter.

STOCK:

Heads, tails, bones, skin
2 sliced carrots
2 teaspoons salt
6 cups cold water.

2 sliced onions
2 sliced celery stalks
1/2 teaspoon pepper

Spoon sliced vegetables over fish heads, etc, already in pot. Sprinkle with salt and pepper and place fish balls on top. Add water, cover pot and bring to quick boil. When water boils, remove cover, reduce heat and simmer 2 hours. Transfer fish to serving platter and strain stock over top.

BORDEN LAKE SOUR CREAMED WHITEFISH

large whitefish   *1/4 cup chopped onion*
1/2 cup diced celery   *2 tablespoons bacon fat*
2 tablespoons grated lemon rind *1/2 teaspoon salt*
1/2 teaspoon paprika   *1/4 cup sour cream*
2 1/2 cups soft bread crumbs

Cook onion, celery and butter for 5 minutes. Blend lemon rind, salt and paprika into sour cream. Add soft bread and mixed well. Pour onions and celery over mixture and stir until blended. Stuff fish and bake at 350°F for 20 minutes.

PEFFERLAW BEER BATTERED WHITEFISH

4 pounds whitefish fillets   *1 1/2 cups all purpose flour*
1 teaspoon salt   *1 1/2 cups beer*
2 eggs   *cooking oil*

Place flour in deep bowl. Beat egg until frothy. Add salt, beer and egg to flour. Beat until free of lumps. Coat each fillet separately and drip off excess. Carefully deep fry in hot oil until light brown. Serve hot with lemon slices.

ORANGE BUTTER WHITEFISH

2 pounds whitefish fillets   *3 tablespoons melted butter*
2 tablespoons orange juice   *1/2 teaspoon salt*
3 orange slices, halved   *parsley*
1 tablespoon coarsely grated orange rind

Divide whitefish into 3 or 4 servings. Place on a well-greased bake and serve platter. Combine melted butter, orange juice and salt. Pour over fillets. Sprinkle with coarsely grated orange rind. Bake at 450 degrees until cooked. Serve garnished with orange slices and parsley.

LAKE SIMCOE TOMATO STUFFED WHITEFISH

4 to 5 pounds cleaned whole whitefish
1/2 teaspoon poultry seasoning   *4 cups soft bread cubes*
1/3 cup chopped onion   *1/3 cup diced celery*
3 tablespoons butter   *1 medium chopped tomato*
1 teaspoon salt   *4 cups soft bread cubes*

Cook onion and celery in butter until tender. Add cooked vegetables and seasonings to bread and toss lightly. Stuff and close fish. Bake for 20 minutes at 350°F. Serve with white wine.

SMELTS

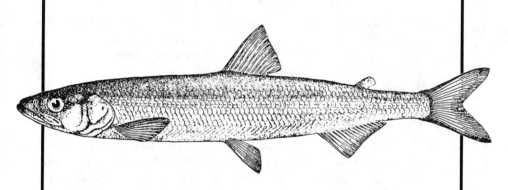

These tasty little fish inhabit the North Pacific and Atlantic oceans as well as the Great Lakes and have been stocked in the reservoirs in the Missouri River basin. While smelt can be enticed to the hook, most are captured during their spawning run with a seine or dip nets used after dark. The annual spring spawning runs of the Great Lakes attract tens of thousands of anglers in pursuit of the tasty little critters.

GREAT LAKES HOOLIGAN SMELT

20 smelt
1 tablespoon salt
1 cup milk

3/4 cup flour
3/4 cup dry bread crumbs

Clean smelt by removing heads and viscera. Wash and drain. Add salt to milk. Blend flour and crumbs together. Dip smelt in milk and then into flour mixture. Fry in hot fat until smelt are brown on one side. Turn smelt carefully and brown other side. Drain on absorbent paper and serve with lemon wedges.

FORT ERIE SMELT AND TOMATO FRY

2 pounds smelt
1 egg, beaten
2 tablespoons milk
1 cup dry bread crumbs
2 tablespoons finely chopped parsley

4 large sliced tomatoes
1 teaspoon sugar
1 teaspoon salt

Clean and wash smelt with head, tail and insides removed. Combine eggs with milk and salt. Dip fish in egg mixture and roll in crumbs. Pan fry in hot fat. When fish are brown on one side, turn and brown on other side. Drain and keep hot on a heated platter. In a clean frying pan, heat 2 tablespoons of fat and add tomato slices, sugar and salt. Fry in hot fat for 1 minute on each side. Sprinkle with chopped parsley and place on platter with fish and serve immediately.

Makes 5 to 6 servings and is excellent with cold beer.

CRYSTAL BEACH SMELT FRY

4 pounds smelt
8 tablespoons lemon juice

1 cup flour
1 cup cream

Clean smelt, removing head and tail. Season with lemon juice and allow to stand for 1 hour. Dip smelt in cream and roll in flour. Lower into hot oil and allow to cook for 4 to 5 minutes.

FAST FRY SMELT

2 pounds smelt

salt, pepper and garlic

Drop cleaned smelt in hot oil for 2 to 4 minutes. Drain and serve. Sprinkle with seasoning and enjoy.

SMELT BAKE FANTASTIC

30 smelt
1 finely chopped clove of garlic
1 cup whole milk

1 finely chopped onion
1/2 cup cracker crumbs
salt and pepper to taste.

Clean and wash smelt. Place smelt in a well greased casserole. Sprinkle garlic, onion, salt and pepper over fish. Cover with a 1/4 inch layer of cracker crumbs. Continue layers until smelt are used. Pour milk over all. Bake in oven at 350 degrees for 1 hour.

SMELT DELIGHT

15 smelt, cleaned with heads removed
1/4 cup finely grated green peppers
8 tablespoons of butter
1/2 cup chopped celery
1/4 teaspoon white pepper
1 teaspoon dried parsley flakes

1/2 cup bread crumbs
1/2 cup white wine
salt to taste

Butter the bottom of a small baking dish. Mix lightly into the dish parsley flakes, celery and green peppers. Arrange smelt on top. Sprinkle smelt with bread crumbs, salt and pepper. Place a half teaspoon of butter on each smelt. Bake in oven at 450 degrees for 10 to 12 minutes. At the 5 minute mark baste smelt with liquid from bottom of dish.

PORT DOVER BROILED SMELT

20 smelt with heads removed *salt and pepper to taste*
1 cup flour *8 tablespoons melted butter*
3 tablespoons lemon juice

Mix lemon juice, butter, salt and pepper thoroughly. Dip each smelt in butter mixture and roll in flour. Place on broiler rack and broil for 5 minutes. Turn once.

JOSHUA'S CREEK SMELT WITH BROWN GRAVY

20 smelt *1 1/2 teaspoon salt*
2 slices of lemon *1 pint of boiling water*
2 tablespoons of shortening *2 tablespoons flour*

Fillet smelt. Roll each fillet and fasten with toothpicks. Place smelt rolls in saucepan. Add 1 teaspoon salt and lemon slices to boiling water and pour over smelt. Simmer fish for 10 minutes until smelt flake easily with fork. Put smelt on a hot plate. Melt shortening in a saucepan and blend in salt, remaining flour and stir until brown. Add liquid from smelt boil. Stir until smooth. Cover smelt with gravy and serve hot.

CHIPS AND SMELT

30 smelt *2 cups vegetable oil*
1 cup finely ground potato chips *3 eggs*

Clean smelt and remove heads. Beat eggs. Dip smelt into egg mix. Remove excess egg and roll smelt in potato chips. Deep fry in hot oil until smelt are cooked. Serve with lemon wedges.

FISH SAUCES

Various fish sauces can be easily prepared that will transform an average fish dinner into a culinary delight.

DILL SAUCE

2 uncooked egg yolks
1 cup salad oil
1 tablespoon dry mustard
1 teaspoon dill seed
1/2 cup wipping cream
1/4 teaspoon worcestershire sauce

2 hardboiled egg yolks
1 1/2 tablespoons vinegar
1/4 teaspoon pepper
1/2 teaspoon salt

Squeeze hard boiled egg yolks through a sieve. Mix with uncooked yolks and beat slowly into salad oil. Add vinegar slowly to avoid curdling. Combine worcestershire sauce, mustard, salt and pepper. Before serving fold in whipped cream and add dill seed.

BÉARNAISE SAUCE

2 egg yolks
2 tablespoons parsley
3 1/2 tablespoons lemon juice
1 tablespoon tarragon vinegar

1/2 cup butter
1/2 teaspoon tarragon

In a saucepan stir lemon juice and egg yolks. Add half the butter and stir over low heat. Once that butter is melted, add the remainder of the butter. As you stir, be sure butter melts slowly so that the eggs cook and the sauce thickens without curdling. Add parsley, tarragon and tarragon vinegar.

DRAWN BUTTER SAUCE

No sauce is as simple to prepare as Drawn Butter Sauce. Melt butter slowly over a low heat source or in the top of a double boiler.

SIOUX LOOKOUT HERBED TOMATO SAUCE

2 cups tomato purée
1 teaspoon salt
2 tablespoons cornflour
4 tablespoons chopped parsley

1/2 teaspoon thyme
1/2 teaspoon pepper
1 teaspoon sugar
4 tablespoons water

Heat tomato purée, oregano, sugar, salt and pepper in a small saucepan. As the ingredients come to a boil, mix in cornflour and cold water to make a sauce. Add chopped parsley and serve sauce hot over any Ontario trout, pike, salmon, perch or bass.

STEELHEADER'S TARTAR SAUCE

2 cups mayonnaise
1 medium onion
1 teaspoon prepared mustard
3 tablespoons chopped olives

4 tablespoons sweet relish
2 tablespoons parsley
1 teaspoon chopped chives

Mix all ingredients and serve with salmon, steelhead, perch or walleye.

SWEET AND SOUR FISH SAUCE

1 1/2 tablespoons cornstarch
1 cube beef bouillion
2/3 cup catsup
1/8 teaspoon garlic powder

1/2 cup vinegar
1/2 cup boiling water
1/2 cup sugar

Slowly mix vinegar and cornstarch until smooth. Dissolve beef cube in boiling water and combine all ingredients. Cook over medium heat and stir constantly until thick and smooth. Cook 10 minutes.

FRENCH CANADIAN SOUR CREAM SAUCE

2 tablespoons chopped onions
3 tablespoons butter
1 cup sour cream
4-ounce can of drained sliced mushrooms

3 tablespoons flour
1/2 teaspoon lemon pepper
3/4 cup salmon liquid

Slowly cook onions in butter until tender. Mix in flour and seasonings and stir until smooth. Cook and as it thickens blend in salmon liquid. Add mushrooms and sour cream. Cook until mildly hot.

BELLEVILLE CREAMED CURRY SAUCE

4 tablespoons butter
2 tablespoons flour
3 teaspoons curry powder

2 cups milk
2 tablespoons minced onion

Melt butter and add minced onions, cooking until tender. Stir in curry powder and flour. Slowly add hot milk to this mixture, continually stirring until it boils. Strain and serve with hot fish.

GEORGIAN BAY CHEDDAR SAUCE

4 tablespoons butter
1/2 cup shredded cheddar

2 1/2 tablespoons flour
1 1/2 cup milk

In a small saucepan, melt butter and blend in flour. Cook for 1 minute. Remove from heat and add milk. Return to low heat and stir until thick and smooth. Add cheese and stir until melted. Serve hot.

SHANTY BAY MUSHROOM SAUCE

1 cup sliced fresh mushrooms
4 tablespoons butter
2 slightly beaten egg yolks
2 cups water

4 tablespoons flour
2 bouillion cubes
1/2 teaspoon salt
1/2 teaspoon nutmeg

Melt butter and brown mushroom slices. Blend in flour and add bouillion cubes, water and seasonings. Stir a small amount of the sauce into egg yolk and then back into remaining sauce. Serve hot.

SOUPS & CHOWDERS

Soups, stews and chowders are easy to prepare and delicious besides. Just about all North American game fish will go fine in the chowder pot. Experiment and you might be surprised.

WISCONSIN ANGLER'S WALLEYE CHOWDER

3 cups boneless walleye fillets   *1/2 cup chopped celery*
1 chopped onion   *8 strips bacon*
1 can cream of potato soup   *1 1/2 cups milk*
2 tablespoons butter   *pinch of parsley flakes*
salt , pepper and other seasonings to taste

Boil walleye fillets with celery and onions in a small amount of water. Drain when cooked. Fry bacon until crisp. Crumble bacon and combine all ingredients, seasoning to taste. Boil for 3 minutes then simmer for 20 minutes, stirring continuously.

GREAT LAKE'S WHITEFISH CHOWDER

2 1/2 cups flaked raw fish
3 onions, finely chopped
1 1/4 pints milk
1/4 teaspoon parsley

8 small potatoes
1/2 pound fat salt pork
2 1/2 cups boiling water
1/4 teaspoon marjoram

Fry up pork in a deep pot and when done remove. Add fish, marjoram, parsley, onions and potatoes to the pot. Cover the ingredients with boiling water and simmer for 1/2 hour. Add milk, salt and pepper and continue to cook for an additional 7 minutes.

FISHERMAN'S TROUT CHOWDER

1 15 1/2-ounce can trout
2 3/4 cups trout liquid and milk, combined
2 medium potatoes, peeled, cooked and cubed
1/4 cup butter or margarine
1/4 cup onion, chopped
1/2 teaspoon salt
1 bay leaf

3 tablespoons flour
dash pepper
1 tablespoon parsley

Drain trout, remove skin and bones, and reserve liquid; break into chunks. Add milk to trout liquid to equal 2 3/4 cups. In a 3-quart saucepan melt butter and saute onion; blend in flour, salt and pepper; add milk/trout liquid mixture and bay leaf. Cook and stir until thickened and bubbly. Add trout chunks, potatoes and parsley. Heat through. Serves 4

ERIE BEACH COHO CHOWDER

3 pounds diced coho salmon   *6 large potatoes*
2 large chopped onions   *1/4 pound butter*
13-ounce can evaporated milk
salt and pepper to taste

Cover potatoes and onions with water 1/2 inch over potatoes. Simmer for 20 minutes. Add diced coho and salt, simmering for 15 minutes. Add butter, pepper and evaporated milk and simmer for another 20 minutes.

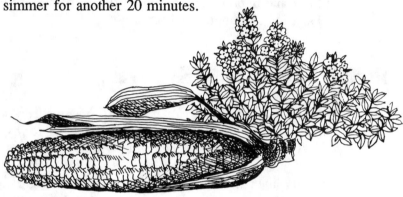

WASAGA BEACH STEELHEAD CHOWDER

2 1/2 cups cooked and flaked rainbow trout
8 ounce can of whole corn kernels
1 cup boiling water   *1 chicken bouillon cube*
1/4 cup margarine   *1/2 cup chopped onions*
16 ounce can tomatoes   *1/4 cup green peppers*
1/2 teaspoon salt   *1/2 teaspoon thyme*
dash pepper

Dissolve bouillon cube in boiling water. In another skillet melt butter and cook onions and peppers until tender. Combine all ingredients and cook on low heat for approximately 15 minutes to blend flavours.

SAUBLE CHINOOK CHOWDER

2 cups flaked chinook
1/4 cup chopped onions
1/2 teaspoon salt
1 bay leaf
2 peeled, cooked and cubed potatoes

2 1/2 cups milk
3 tablespoons flour
dash pepper
1 tablespoon parsley

In a 3 quart saucepan melt butter and saute onions. Blend in flour, pepper and salt in with milk and bay leaf. Cook and stir until thick and bubbling. Add salmon flakes, parsley and potatoes. Heat for 15 minutes and serve hot.

PORT SEVERN PIKE STEW

3 pounds of cut up pike
cayenne pepper
6 pounds potatoes, cleaned, cut into 1/4 inch slices

8 to 10 bacon slices
salt and pepper to taste

Alternately layer fish and potatoes in a large baking dish ending with potatoes on top. Dot each layer of fish with butter. Place bacon across top with cayenne pepper. Cover with water and slow cook until tender. Allow top to brown. This recipe is also excellent with bass, musky or salmon.

DUNNVILLE CATFISH STEW

6 pounds Grand River channel cat fillets
1 pint milk
pinch sage
4 tablespoons butter

pinch marjoram
4 tablespoons onion
salt and pepper to taste

Soak catfish fillets in salt water for 1 1/2 hours. Boil fish and salt water for 10 minutes. Drain off water and add remaining ingredients to fish and simmer for 15 minutes.

SMOKING IS GOOD FOR YOUR HEALTH

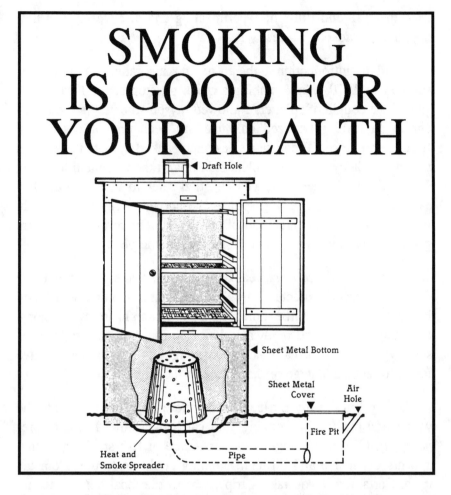

Most say that smoking is bad for your health. On that statement I have to agree, but also disagree. Sure I hate to see the better half puffing away on those sticks of rolled tobacco. Even worse I shudder when I think of the thousand dollars or more of fishing tackle I could invest in if I could re-direct the greenbacks from her hourly habit. But the smoking of a king salmon, steelhead, brown trout or lake trout, now that's a completely different matter. Nothing but nothing is as delicious as a fillet of properly smoked salmonid. Come to think of it, nothing but nothing is quite as tasty as a properly smoked smallmouth bass, smelt, catfish or perch either. I've tried them all and I'm still experimenting and discovering just how appetizing smoked fish really is.

I had my introduction to the art of smoking game fish back in the summer of 1970. While making a quick pit stop at the local tackle shop for a couple of spinners I allowed myself to be talked into purchasing a little galvanized box that has been one of my closest friends ever since. Of course a sales pitch backed up with the aid of a tray full of juicy lake trout fillets didn't harm the presentation either. That little galvanized box, as I so often refer to it, has more than earned its cherished resting spot in the corner of my basement. In fact, it now has the companionship of two similar containers. All are given steady employment twelve months of the year.

By now you probably realize that I'm speaking of my Little Chief Smoker. Manufactured by the Luhr Jensen Company of Hood River, Oregon. The Little Chief is a common sight in tackle shops, department stores and hardware chains across the country. What is surprising is the fact that a large percentage of Ontario anglers have failed to take advantage of the values of the Little Chief.

Before I praise my Little Chief anymore let's first delve into the values and method of smoking your catch over other forms of preparing fish. To many anglers the procedure of fish smoking at first appears expensive and difficult. Nothing could be further from the truth. Certainly, if you take a trip down to the local deli a vacuum packed portion of smoked trout or salmon is just about beyond the reach of us average mortals on a regular basis. But under many circumstances homemade smokehouses are inexpensive and simple to construct. At first it may require a small degree of experimenting to discover just how well you prefer your fish brined and cooked, but the steps toward success actually are very simple.

Smoking your catch includes first a salting or infusion of salt in to the fish. Called 'curing', this is a simple process that causes the fish to undergo certain physical, chemical and bacteriological changes which result in greatly extended stability. More specifically, salt (sodium chloride) acts to suppress the growth of spoilage causing bacteria and to solubize the available meat proteins. With the introduction of salt to a cut of fish, the fish proteins dissolve and the fish becomes tacky. When heated, the dissolved proteins set up and 'bind' the fish. This phenomena is most important in the manufacture of dried fish products.

There are two methods of smoking—Hot Smoking and Cold Smoking. With the favoured hot smoking method the fish is completely smoked and flavoured at 160 to 180 degrees. Although a hot smoked product will not keep more than a few days without refrigeration or freezing it is the most popular and easiest form of smoking and the method we will discuss in this article. It is also the shortest of the two methods to carry out. Cold smoking is left most often to the commercial large scale operators.

THE COVER BRINE AND SMOKE

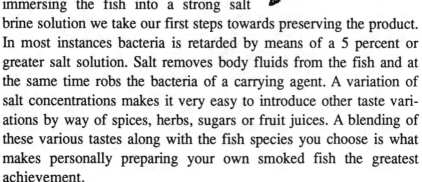

The science and art of 'curing' is simply the infusion of salt into your food products. The simplest method of curing fish is by means of the Cover Brine. By immersing the fish into a strong salt brine solution we take our first steps towards preserving the product. In most instances bacteria is retarded by means of a 5 percent or greater salt solution. Salt removes body fluids from the fish and at the same time robs the bacteria of a carrying agent. A variation of salt concentrations makes it very easy to introduce other taste variations by way of spices, herbs, sugars or fruit juices. A blending of these various tastes along with the fish species you choose is what makes personally preparing your own smoked fish the greatest achievement.

In the smokehouse the smoke invades the flesh of the fish adding not only flavour to the product, but also adds tensile strength to the meat tissues of the fish. It is imperative that too much heat not be added to the fish before the smoke can achieve its curing action. Smoke firms up the flesh of the fish and with the proper degree of heat dehydrates the product.

Under proper conditions the smoker should (1) remove moisture quickly; (2) raise internal temperature of your product to approximately 165 degrees; and (3) finally, provide an efficient and reliable smoke generated that supplies old-fashioned smoke flavour to the fish of your choice.

THE SMOKEHOUSE

Now to decide on your choice of smoker. As I've mentioned I love my Little Chief, but there will be more on that later. If you live in commercial fish country along the shores of Lake Erie, Huron, Superior or Georgian Bay, you soon realize that the old timers love abandoned refrigerators to convert into personal smokehouses. I am presently on the lookout for a suitable icebox that I can convert into a smoker for the big volume preparation of salmon. I am familiar with other anglers who have used a simple inverted wine keg to act as a smoker. Then again, in a pinch it's easy to convert a sturdy cardboard box into a mini-smokehouse.

Glenn Osborne, an ex-charter boat operator from Bronte, fished under the title of the 'Salmon Smoker' and for good reason. Osborne had constructed a brick smoke house in the front porch of his home. Others have constructed steel frame or brick smokers that are more than adequate.

Remember that you are not out to fast cook your salmon. A combination of the proper brine, temperature (165 degrees Fahrenheit) and smoke is the answer. Just enough draft should be present to allow the proper amount of smoke to escape. Just the right amount of heat should be applied to reach that 165 degrees and at the same time produce the smoke.

I'm acquainted with a number of anglers who have devised various smokers of their own design. For the most part they are happy with the performance of these inventions. Remember though, don't expect to work miracles with your home built smokehouse. It will take a little or more than a little experimenting to get the process down pat.

CHOOSING THE BEST WOOD

It's impossible to smoke your catch without a source of smoke. Although I've noticed smoke powder on the market in the past I would suggest that you only choose natural wood or another form of Mother Nature's finest. Hickory, Alder, Cherry and Apple chips. Again, it's up to the artist to experiment. Probably the finest smoked fish (besides my own) that I've ever tasted was cooked up by a Brantford friend, Jim Styres. Styres magic brew was heated and smoked with the aid of dried corn cobs. Chips and sawdust of the wood are the only way to create your smoke. Be certain that bark is not included as part of the fuel.

It should be noted at this time that a smoker is not an instrument of magic. It cannot restore freshness and good flavour to food that is already tainted. Salmon that is already into the spawning stage, dark and with deteriorating flesh is best left to the garbage. That same holds true to the spawning steelhead of spring. Never dump that dark spawner in the garbage bin, but instead leave the fish to spawn and then return to the open lake.

Before preparing the fish for the brine be certain that the fillet is free of all blood. If the steaking or chunk style of cut is required be certain that large bones are removed and that chunks are cut small enough to handle easily. Depending on the size of your smoker it is possible that whole fish can be prepared. In this case the head can be left on. Be certain that the kidney is completely removed when cleaning.

MY LITTLE CHIEF

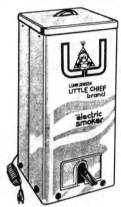

As I've mentioned I patronize my Little Chief. In fact, all three of them. Wood chips are heated by means of small electrical element in the bottom and the enclosed instruction book has been devised to make the various recipes fool proof. I've smoked everything from barracuda, to turkey, to peanuts in these units. Best of all hundreds of trout, salmon and bass have been prepared without loss or spoilage in my Little Chief. I've also been able to experiment with my own brines. That smoked salmon always seems to taste a whole lot better when I've been able to utilize my own 'secret' mixture of wine, honey, brown sugar and even garlic.

When the gang drops in they might find a chicken resting in the brine and salmon fillets on the rack. Then again, they might be served up a portion of Jiffy Smoked Fish Patties or a sampling of my Georgian Bay King Salmon Sausages. Although as I mentioned I am venturing into a large scale homemade smoker in the future I'll continue to use the three Little Chiefs.

Better still is the compact size of the Little Chief. Only three feet in height, fourteen inches in width and fourteen inches in depth, this little wonder is capable of smoking up to a duo of whole salmon or two complete steaked kings. The Little Chief is light enough and small enough to store in a closet and can be used both winter and summer. Unless you are planning on smoking up salmon and trout on a large scale, the Little Chief will be more than adequate for all your needs.

During a trip to Oregon back in the early 70s I arrived early and unannounced at the Luhr Jensen plant that is located along the shores of the Columbia River. Up on the flat roof of the building I found Jensen promotions manager Buzz Ramsey watching over a pair of Little Chiefs that were giving off the sweet aroma of smouldering cherry wood. One unit was filled to the brim with the chunky steaks of two adult steelhead. The other smoker was preparing a delicacy that Ramsey referred to as 'Indian Candy'. That candy was nothing more than the skeleton, ribs and a small amount of clinging flesh that remained of the two steelhead that had furnished the meat for the first smoker. The finished product from both units proved to be excellent and even though pickings were a little slim in the second smoker Ramsey's example illustrated that we should never take for granted or abuse our fish stocks.

In my profession I have the opportunity to converse with, as well as observe other anglers here in Ontario. A major concern of mine is that most sportsmen fail to utilize our valuable fish stocks once they are placed on the stringer. To a true angler there should be no crime worse than to waste what Nature has provided us. The smokehouse technique allows the angler to prepare his catch in a thousand exciting and delicious ways.

Remember, the art of smoking is not difficult. Instead it's fascinating and exciting.

Further information:
- *"Little Chief Electric Smoker Book"*, send $2.00 to Luhr Jensen and Sons, 524 Powell St., Vancouver, B.C. V6A 1G9
- *"Smoking Salmon & Trout"*, Jack Whelan, Aerie Publishing, Deep Bay, RR#1, Bowser, B.C. V0R 1G0
- *"Keeping the Catch"*, Kenn Oberrecht, Winchester Press, P.O. Box 1260, Tulsa, Oklahoma 74101

LITTLE CHIEF SMOKED SALMON DELUXE (Chinook, Coho, etc.)

Brine:

1/3 cup sugar	*1/4 cup non-iodized salt*
2 cups soy sauce	*1 cup water*
1/2 teaspoon onion powder	*1/2 teaspoon garlic powder*
1/2 teaspoon pepper	*1/2 teaspoon tabasco sauce*
1 cup dry white wine	

Brine salmon chunks 8 or more hours, keeping refrigerated. Fill flavour pan with Hickory, Alder, or mix 2/3 Apple with 1/3 Cherry. Use 2 to 3 panfuls. Leave in the smoker until drying is completed. This may take 12 hours, depending on the thickness of the meat. Place largest and thickest chunks on the bottom rack. (Also use for Steelhead and other large trout.)

EASY CURE SMOKED FISH

1 quart water   *1/2 cup white sugar*
1/2 cup non-iodized salt

Fill a quart jar 1/2 full with good warm water. Add salt and sugar. Mix well until dissolved. Top off jar with cold water. This recipe may be increased if you need more brine.

Immerse prepared fish chunks, filets or small whole fish completely in the brine solution. Brine chunks 1" thick, 8 to 12 hours or overnight. Brine filets to 1/2" thick about 4 hours and small whole fish or very thin pieces about 2 to 4 hours. Stir solution and rotate fish occasionally. Remove from brine. Rinse each piece in cool water and place on paper towels. Pat dry. In about 1 hour, you will notice a tacky glaze on the surface of the fish. This is called the "pellicle". Your fish is now ready for loading into the smoker.

THICK CHUNKS—Smoke 8 to 12 hours, using 3 panfuls of Chips 'n Chunks flavour fuel.
FILETS TO 1/2"—Smoke 5 to 8 hours, using 2 panfuls of Chips 'n Chunks flavour fuel.
SMALL FISH, THIN PIECES—Smoke 2 to 4 hours, using 1 or 2 panfuls of Chips n' Chunks flavour fuel. Add Chips 'n Chunks during early stages of the drying cycle. Check the meat periodically for the degree of doneness you desire.

SMOKED SALMON AND CREAM CHEESE OMELET

Saute 2 chopped green onions and 1/3 cup smoked salmon in butter for 2 or 3 minutes. Stir in cubed cream cheese (3 oz. package) until melted. Use to fill two 3-egg omelets.

LITTLE CHIEF SMOKED FISH #2
(for oily fish with a stronger flavour)

2 quarts water
1 cup non-iodized salt
1/2 cup brown sugar
2 tablespoon lemon concentrate or 1/4 cup lemon juice

1/4 tablespoon garlic powder
1/4 tablespoon onion powder

Use small fish or filet of large. Mix all ingredients and stir until dissolved. Brine fish 4 or more hours. Rinse and dry. Rack and load. Use 3 to 5 panfuls Hickory, Apple or Alder. Keep in the smoker 4 to 10 hours, depending on the size of fish pieces.

(Use this recipe for: Cod, Bass, Pike, Tuna types, Sturgeon, Barracuda, Mackerel, Eels, and for Squid and Octopus.)

JIFFY SMOKED FISH PATTIES

2 cups flaked fish (canned or left overs)
1 cup bread crumbs or crackers (smoked if you like)
2 beaten eggs   dash pepper
1 tablespoon minced onion   salt to taste

Place fish in a greased baking dish that will fit into your "Little Chief", spreading evenly and loosely in the dish. Smoke for 1 panful of Hickory or Alder Chips 'n Chunks flavour fuel and allow to cool.

Mix ingredients thoroughly. Mold into patties and fry in hot butter or bacon grease until golden brown. These are great on toast with white sauce, or make a smoked fishburger with all the trimmings. Yum!

SMOKEY SALMON NUGGETS

2 cups flaked, smoked salmon   *1 egg, beaten slightly*
1 tsp grated onion   *dash pepper*
1/2 cup fine cornflake crumbs   *oil for deep-fat frying*
1 1/2 cups seasoned mashed potatoes

Combine fish, potatoes, egg, onion and pepper. Beat until smooth. Chill well. Portion fish mixture with a 1/4 cup measure. Shape into balls. Roll in crumbs. Fry in hot, deep fat, 350°F, 3 to 5 minutes or until thoroughly heated and lightly browned. Serve hot with your favourite egg or cheese sauce. Makes 12 balls. Approximately 4 servings.

LITTLE CHIEF SMOKEY SMELT
(the beer-drinker's friend)

Brine:
1 cup non-iodized salt   *1 cup brown sugar*
1 cup soy sauce   *1/2 cup cider vinegar*
1 tablespoon paprika   *1 tablespoon chili powder*
1 tablespoon onion salt   *1/2 teaspoon pepper*
1 tablespoon Worcestershire sauce
1 tablespoon garlic salt (optional)
3 cups warm water

Some prefer whole smelt, others remove heads and entrails with a pair of scissors. Either way, wash smelt in clear water. Mix all ingredients in warm water. Let the brine cool and add the smelt. Brine the smelt 4 or more hours. Rinse and air dry.

Use 3 panfuls of Apple, Alder or Hickory flavour fuel. Keep in the smoker until done. (5 to 7 hours.)

CANNING

Tell me honestly. What do you do with all those big trout and salmon you catch?

Chances are you eat the majority or at least half of your annual catch. Then again, if you troll away most of your summer days for kings and coho or are lucky enough to hit the rainbow rivers often enough some of those fish might be going to waste. You can't count on the freezer to come to your rescue. Freezers are great for short term storage, but even properly packaged, salmonids lose a lot of their quality after a couple of months in the deep freeze. I seldom give fish away anymore. I've found that unless they've angled for them, a lot of recipients often tuck these donations in the back of the freezer and let them collect a wasteful dose of frostburn.

I've discovered that canning is the best way for preserving my catch, whether it be coho, king, brown, brook, lake or rainbow trout. If you have yet to enjoy Lomi Lomi Stuffed Tomatoes, Steelhead Archiduc, Chinook a la King, Lake Trout Pancakes or a Fluffy Fisherman's Steelhead Omelet you just haven't lived. In fact, if you've never had the opportunity to climb into the E-Z chair on a cold winter's evening, pop the lid on 1/2 pint and dig directly into a jar of your own canned salmon, you are missing out on one of the greatest delights that can be derived from the sport of angling.

My first encounter with canned salmon, other than the commercial product one can purchase at the local A & P, came about back in 1971 on the far side of the Rocky Mountains. I was enjoying a fishing vacation for chinook and steelhead with Luhr Jensen's promo director Buzz Ramsey. If it's one thing that Ramsey and all other anglers have in common along the streams of the Pacific Northwest, it was that no fish, big or small, was ever to be wasted. Out in big water country they smoke 'm, fry 'm, poach 'm, and cann 'm. Most often they cann 'm.

I believe that over a 14 day period I consumed more trout and salmon than I had in my previous 20 years. I had salmon scrambled eggs for breakfast, salmon patties for lunch and salmon casserole for supper. I even had salmon seafood potpourri salad for a late night snack. Besides heading back to Ontario with 10 extra pounds under my belt, I also brought an addiction for canned salmon.

In his role as head of promotions and outside sale for one of North America's largest fishing tackle corporations, Buzz Ramsey plays host to hundreds of members of the industry and outdoor press annually. This angling expert and his guests beach thousands of salmonids annually and although most are released to fight another day, enough are killed to be shipped home with his visitors or for his own use. On the first day of my arrival I caught sight of a 5 foot high stack of cartons, each of which contained a dozen half pint jars of rich canned salmon or steelhead.

Besides picking up on the West Coast methods for catching trout and salmon, I was allowed to assist Buzz in preparing my own 3 cartons of half pint jars for my trip back to Ontario. I discovered that not only was the technique simple to carry out, but also when completed I had prepared salmon and trout that would keep indefinitely and also allow me to serve my catch in a hundred different recipes.

As I've mentioned, the canning of fish is simple. The most important aspect of this method of preparation is to follow the few rules of canning to the letter.

I've heard tell of anglers canning their catch in open lidded pots and preserving pans. To those anglers I can only wish them luck and hope they have their OHIP payments up to date. The only 'safe' way to can any fish is with the aid of a **pressure cooker**. When canning your catch follow the directions in your canner manual closely to protect against spoilage.

Whenever possible I attempt to can fish that are absolutely fresh. As soon as the fish is caught I kill it and place it on ice. Cleaning your fish is next important stage. When canning any salmonid I completely fillet my catch. This includes removing all bone, skin, blood and belly fat. In order to draw out all blood before canning, place the fish in a brine made in the proportions of 1 oz. salt to a quart of water. The fish is allowed to soak from 10 minutes to 1 hour. The fish is then removed from the brine, drained well and cut into jar lengths. The jars used are either 1/2 pint or pint mason jars equipped with rubber snap lids. The fish strips are packed closely in the jar to within 1/4 inch from the top. A small amount of salt (1/2 teaspoon to the 1/2 pint jar, 1 teaspoon to the pint jar) is added to the top of the fish. Before placing on the lids and sealing by hand be certain that the top of the glass jars are completely free of fish, salt or any other foreign matter that may prevent the lid from sealing to the jar. Hand seal the rubber lids and rings to the glass jars.

From here on it's a simple case of following the instructions that come with the pressure cooker. I usually fill the cooker with 2 to 3 inches of water, place in the first rack and fill the rack with jars. Depending on the size of your cooker a second rack can be added and another layer of jars placed in the cooker. Next securely tighten down the lid of the cooker and turn on the heat. After the steam begins to build, close the escape valve and regulate the pressure control on the lid at a constant 10 pounds. It is important that timing begins once the control reaches the 10 pound mark. Process at this pressure setting for 90 minutes.

At the end of the cooking time, remove the pressure cooker from the heat and allow the pressure to reduce normally. Hastening this draw down period will only result in broken seals on the jars. Once the pressure reading has fallen to 0 remove the jars from the pressure cooker. Hand tighten the jars once more. It is important to label and date all jars for later stock inventory.

Presently I have six cases of canned salmon and trout tucked safely away in a corner of the Ontario Fisherman storeroom. Those 72 half pint jars represent 5 adult chinook salmon caught in Owen Sound Bay last summer. Rosy red in colour, I pass out those same half pint jars to friends and acquaintances on special occasions. I have yet to have one recipient turn down the offer of a jar, or for that matter not remark that the salmon or trout was fantastic. With a family of four under our roof, I always attempt to keep one person's limit of trout and salmon in jars.

Upon making that return trip from the West Coast back in 1971 I stopped off at the first Sears department store I came across and purchased an All-American 910 pressure cooker. That pressure cooker can adequately handle 16 half pint jars in one process. On another occasion I happened across a similar cooker at a flea market. With the two cookers I can usually prepare a one person day's limit of big chinook salmon or steelhead in approximately four hours. That four hours of cooking can be proportioned out over the span of year. As noted, right out of the jar on crackers or served up in a hundred other recipes, canned salmon is simple to prepare, yet fantastic to eat.

Resources:
All-American Pressure Cookers are made by Wisconsin Aluminum Foundry Co. Inc., P.O. Box 246, Manitowoc, Wisconsin, U.S.A. 54220

STEELHEAD ARCHIDUC

2 cups cooked & flaked or one 15 1/2-ounce can of steelhead
4 1/2 cups combined* steelhead liquid & milk

1/4 cup minced onion	*1/4 cup melted butter*
2 tablespoons flour	*1/2 teaspoon salt*
1/4 teaspoon pepper	*dash cayenne*
1/2 cup heavy cream	*1/4 cup sherry*
2 tablespoons cognac	*Toast or rice*

1 tablespoon finely chopped parsley

If using canned steelhead, drain, remove skin and bones, and reserve liquid; flake. In a saucepan saute onion in butter until transparent. Stir in flour; remove from heat. Bring milk and steelhead liquid to boil and add to onion mixture. Return to heat stirring constantly until sauce is thick and smooth. Stir in next 6 ingredients. Fold in steelhead and parsley and heat until very hot. Serve on toast. Serves 4.

*If using fresh cooked steelhead, use 4 1/2 cups milk.

CHINOOK A LA KING

one 15 1/2-oz. can salmon   1/2 cup melted butter
1/2 cup chopped celery   1/2 teaspoon salt
1/2 cup chopped green pepper   1/4 cup flour
1 1/2 cups combined salmon liquid and milk
1 cup cooked & sliced mushrooms
2 tablespoons chopped pimento
Patty shell, toast, or cooked rice

Drain salmon, reserving liquid. Melt butter in a pan. Add celery and green pepper; cook until vegetables are tender. Gradually add flour and salt; stir until smooth. Add liquids: cook gently, until sauce is thick and smooth. Add salmon, mushrooms, and pimento. Heat mixture and serve in a patty shell. Serves 6.

LAKE TROUT PANCAKES

1 cup pancake mix   1 egg
1 cup milk   1 tablespoon salad oil
one 7 3/4-ounce can of trout   White Sauce

Combine all ingredients except trout and sauce. Drain and remove skin and bones from trout. Stir batter until smooth; add 1/2 of trout. Heat pancake griddle, oil lightly, and fry each cake until golden brown on both sides. Add remaining trout to a prepared white sauce and serve over hot pancakes. Makes 8 medium cakes. Serves 4.
Note: Sour cream mixed with the remaining lake trout also makes a nice sauce for this dish.

LOMI LOMI STUFFED TOMATOES

one 7 3/4-ounce can salmon *1/2 cup chopped celery*
1/4 cup mayonnaise *6 tomatoes*
1 hard cooked & chopped egg *garnish of lettuce*
1 tablespoon finely chopped onion
1 tablespoon chopped sweet pickle

Drain, remove skin and bones, and flake salmon; combine with next 5 ingredients. Wash tomatoes, cut off tops, and scoop out part of centres. Spoon in salmon filling, piling it high. Serve on a leaf of lettuce. Serves 6.

FLUFFY FISHERMAN'S STEELHEAD OMELET

one 7 3/4-ounce can steelhead *dash oregano*
6 separated eggs *1 tablespoon parsley*
1 teaspoon chopped chives *1/2 teaspoon salt*
2 tablespoons melted butter *dash pepper*
1/3 cup combined steelhead liquid & water

Preheat oven to 350°. Drain steelhead, reserving liquid; flake steelhead. Beat egg whites until stiff. Beat egg yolks until thick and add next 6 ingredients. Add steelhead and mix well. Fold into egg white mixture. Pour omelet mixture into hot, buttered fry pan and cook over low heat for 3 to 5 minutes or until lightly browned. Bake for 2 to 5 minutes or until a knife inserted in the centre comes out clean. Cut part way through centre of omelet and fold in half. Serve immediately on a warm platter. Serves 6.

HOME PICKLING

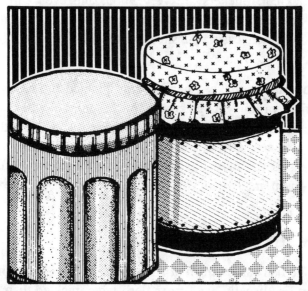

As applied to fish, pickling today generally means a fish product that has been processed with vinegar as an ingredient in the curing process. If this is the first time you have tried pickling fish at home, you will be pleasantly surprised at how easy it is—and what a delight a freshly pickled fish is to eat.

Courtesy of the University of Wisconsin Sea Grant Institute

The size, fat content and flesh of herring make them especially well-suited for pickling, and they are the most common kind of pickled fish sold commercially. Other commercially pickled seafood include salmon, haddock, oysters, sardines, eels, shrimp and clams—but such products are usually sold only as specialty items in small local or ethnic markets.

While the kinds of fish pickled commercially are limited, any fish can be pickled. Northern pike is perhaps one of the best game fish for pickling. Suckers are very good, and even carp are tasty when pickled. The type of fish you use matters only in chunk-style pickling, in which case you should use only thin-skinned, small-boned varieties of fish.

If you want to make a herring-type pickled product with other kinds of fish, various characteristics of the product will be different. Home-pickled fish may not have the same taste or "mouth feel" as that sold commercially. It may be firmer, drier or have a different colour or taste. You may like it more or less than commercially pickled fish—the point is that you shouldn't expect it to be exactly the same.

MAIN INGREDIENTS

Fish — The fish can be fresh or frozen, but it should be of high quality. Frozen fish usually has firmer flesh when pickled than fresh fish due to the tissue disruption caused by freezing and a loss of moisture when the fish is thawed.

Also, the type of fish used will affect the texture and colour of the final pickled product. Fish species differ in bone size and skeletal structure, flesh colour or pigmentation, fat content, the location of fat in the tissues, muscle size, length of muscle and the quantity of muscle.

Water — Good quality (drinking) water should be used to make all brine and spice mixtures. Avoid using "hard" water—especially water high in iron, calcium or magnesium. The presence of these metals in the pickling solution may cause bitter flavours in the pickled fish. If you must use hard water, treat your brine by boiling, cooling and then filtering it through several layers of filter paper, such as coffee filters, to remove any precipitate that forms before using it for pickling.

Vinegar — Use distilled (white) vinegar that is clear, without foreign odors or flavour, and has a guaranteed acetic acid content of at least five percent. The use of vinegar (acetic acid) at the recommended levels will help prevent bacterial growth in the final product. Cider or other fruit vinegars may be used to pickle fish, but the acid content of fruit vinegars is more variable than white vinegar, and fruit flavours and pigments in these vinegars may give the final pickled fish product an off-flavour and colour.

Salt — Use only pure, high-grade granulated pickling or canning salt. The salt used in pickling fish should have low concentrations of calcium, iron and magnesium because, as mentioned above, the presence of these ions may cause bitter flavours as well as undesirable colour changes in the pickled fish. for similar reasons, do not use sea salt, iodized salt or regular table salt.

Sugar — Table (cane or beet) sugar is recommended as the sweetening ingredient in the pickling solution. You may substitute corn syrup for some of the sugar, but be aware that it may add a slight corn flavour and that the sweetness level is more difficult to control. If corn syrup is used, you will have to experiment with the quantity necessary to achieve the desired effect and flavour.

PREPARING THE FISH

Fillet Style — Any species of fish can be used for this type of pickling. Again, the quality of the raw fish used  is a very important factor: use only fish of good quality.

Fillet the fish and remove the skin. Wash the fillets several times with clean, cold water and drain. If the fillets are thick—one inch or thicker—they should be sliced to pieces about 1/2-inch thick.

Fillet Chunks — Use the process described above for pickled fillets. After the fillets have been washed, cut each fillet into chunks about 1 1/2 to 2 inches in length.

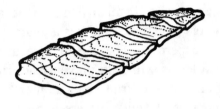

Chunk Style — Chunk-style pickling should only be used with fish with a small bone structure and thin skin—the so-called soft-fleshed fish. Trout, salmon, catfish and similar fish species are not suitable for

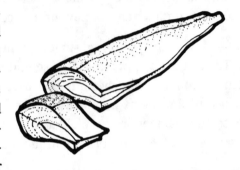

making this type of product because of their thick, tough skin and heavy bones.

To prepare the fish, remove the scales, head, fins and tail. Wash the fish thoroughly in cold water to remove blood, kidney and any visceral material that may remain on the fish surface or in the belly cavity. Cut the cleaned fish into chunks about 1 1/2 inches wide.

BRINING THE FISH

Use a container made of plastic, glass or some other material not affected by salt. Don't use metal containers—salt is corrosive and reacts with various metals.

For each 5 pounds of fish, dissolve 2 1/2 cups of pickling or canning salt in 1 gallon of water. Place the prepared raw fish in the brine and refrigerate for 48 hours. Then rinse the brined fish in cold water and cover with undiluted distilled vinegar, and refrigerate it for another 24 hours. The vinegar soaking further firms the flesh and softens the bones.

After 24 hours, remove the fish from the vinegar and pack it in half-pint or pint jars with chopped onion on the bottom and on the top. Cover with one of the following pickling solutions.

A NOTE OF CAUTION

Some people think that pickled fish can be preserved for longer periods of time if they heat-process the jars in a boiling water bath or use a pressure canner. But boiling water bath or pressure canning of a high-acid and high-sugar product like pickled fish will result in a caramelized, soft-textured and potentially bitter final product. Heat-processing pickled fish is not recommended.

HERRING-STYLE PICKLING
SOLUTION (Treats five pounds of fish)

1 cup dry white wine   5 1/2 cups sugar
1 quart distilled vinegar (5% acetic acid)
4 tablespoons mixed pickling spice (tied in spice bag)

(Before pickling the fish, make sure earlier instructions on preparing and brining are followed.) Combine the vinegar, sugar and spices in a large pan and bring to a boil. Allow it to cool to room temperature. Remove the spice bag. Add the white wine and pour over the packed fish.

Place scalded lids on the jars and refrigerate. Allow it to stand for at least one week before using. This product can be stored in the refrigerator for 6 to 8 weeks.

CREAMED PICKLED FISH VARIATION

After fish have been in the herring-style pickling solution described above for at least a week, pour the pickling solution from the jar into a container. For each pint of fish, place 2 ounces of cultured sour cream in a mixing bowl and add pickling solution until you have enough to refill the jar of fish.

Pour the cream sauce back into the jar and let it stand for 15 to 20 minutes before serving. The creamed fish should be eaten within a few days; if held longer, the cream sauce will separate and curdle.

MUSTARD PICKLING SOLUTION
(Treats five pounds of fish)

1 cup vegetable oil
1/3 cup prepared mustard
3 cups distilled vinegar (5% acetic acid)
1 teaspoon ground white pepper
1 teaspoon mixed pickling spice

1/2 cup sugar
3 bay leaves

Brine the fish in a salt solution and soak in vinegar as described earlier. Rinse and pack the fish in half-point or pint jars with chopped or sliced onion.

Mix listed ingredients in a pan and bring to a boil. Allow mixture to cool to room temperature, then fill the jars of fish with the solution. Cover the jars with scalded lids and refrigerate. Let stand for one week before using. This product can be stored in the refrigerator for 6 to 8 weeks.

LOW IN CALORIES— HIGH IN NUTRITION

Courtesy of the University of Wisconsin Sea Grant Institute

Seafoods have always been held in high esteem as an entrée on restaurant menus, but in recent years an increasing number of people have begun to include more fish and seafood as a regular part of their home menus—and with good reason.

Besides being economical and easy to prepare, fish and seafoods are easy to digest, low in sodium and high in protein, yet contain far fewer calories and less fat than comparable servings of red meats. This has prompted many health- and weight-conscious Canadians to adopt fish and seafoods as true "lean cuisine".

Fish and seafood products are also excellent sources of B-complex vitamins and essential trace minerals, including potassium, iron, phosphorus, copper, iodine, manganese, cobalt and selenium. Fatty species of fish—salmon, whitefish and mackerel, for example—are also rich in vitamins A and D. Some species of shellfish are good sources of zinc and bone-building calcium.

Recent studies indicate that a meal or two of fish each week may also help reduce blood cholesterol levels, a leading cause of atherosclerosis, commonly called hardening of the arteries. Atherosclerosis is a major factor in the development of coronary heart disease, Canada's No. 1 fatal disease.

LOW IN CALORIES

Fish offers high-quality protein with fewer calories than a similar-sized portion of meat (see table). For example, both haddock and ground beef are about 18 percent protein. But the haddock will have only about 22 calories per ounce, while regular ground beef has about 80 calories per ounce.

The total number of calories in a seafood meal depends on your choice of seafood and your method of preparing it. A 3.5-ounce serving of perch, for example, has far fewer calories than an equivalent serving of chinook salmon or sturgeon caviar. And frying, due to the uptake of frying oil, will add more calories to a serving of fish than will broiling, poaching or steaming it. A serving of deep-fried perch, for example, will have far more calories than a similar serving of poached perch.

Condiments like butter and tartar sauce also add a lot of calories to a serving of fish. Dieters can easily avoid the hundreds of calories in tartar sauce and butter by using just a few fresh herbs and spices—such as sweet basil, curry powder or paprika—or a squeeze of lemon or lime juice to enhance the delicate flavours of fish or seafood.

NUTRITIONAL

Doctors and nutritionists nationwide are beginning to recommend more fish and seafoods in the diet, based on scientific research on the beneficial roles of fish and fish oils in human nutrition and general health.

While many aspects of fish and nutrition are still under investigation, much of the current research effort is focused on the various kinds of lipids in fish, particularly the long-chain omega-3 fatty acids, which are unique to fish and fish oils. Trout and salmon in particular are high in omega-3 fatty acids.

Recent research indicates a diet containing fish or fish oils rich in omega-3 fatty acids has beneficial effects on such health problems as hardening of the arteries (atherosclerosis), high levels of cholesterol (blood lipids) and high blood pressure (hypertension), and perhaps even arthritis.

Atherosclerosis, hypertension and obesity are the three major diet-related factors involved in an increased risk of developing coronary heart disease, the cause of nearly half of all deaths in Canada today. On average, one in five Canadians has a problem with atherosclerosis or high blood lipids. A diet generally high in fat content seems to increase blood cholesterol, and a diet high in saturated fats increases blood cholesterol in some people. Seafoods are generally low in cholesterol and fats, and 60 to 80 percent of the fat in seafoods are polyunsaturated fatty acids, like those in vegetable oils.

More than 6 million Canadians suffer from hypertension, and

restriction of the amount of sodium in the diet is often part of the treatment for it. Another important aspect of the dietary management of hypertensive patients is maintaining their potassium levels when certain diuretics are part of the treatment. Freshwater and saltwater species of fish alike are both low in sodium and good sources of potassium. However, the use of brine in processing pickled, smoked and some frozen fish and seafood products can increase the sodium content more than threefold: Read the package label carefully.

Lemon and lime juice are good substitutes for salt in seafood dishes, and tarragon, basil, paprika, garlic, mushrooms and onions all enhance the flavour of seafood dishes without raising the sodium or caloric content significantly.

ECONOMICAL

Besides tasting good and being good for you, fish and seafoods have two other special attractions as home menu items: They are quick and easy to prepare.

Generally speaking, any method used to prepare meat dishes can also be used with seafoods, including baking, broiling, grilling and frying. Unlike many meats, however, fish and other seafoods do not require a lot of cooking to make them tender. In fact, your main concern should be to avoid cooking them too long: Fish steaks and small whole fish can be broiled, steamed, poached or fried in only a few minutes.

And while fish and seafoods generally cost more per pound than red meats, there is little or no bone and fat to trim away and less shrinkage during cooking, so less is wasted.

CALORIE, FAT AND PROTEIN CONTENT OF FISH AND SEAFOODS

This table is based on a 3.5-ounce (100-gram) portion of raw (uncooked) product.

Fish or Seafood	Calories	% Fat	% Protein
Bass (Small & Largemouth)	104	2.6	18.8
Carp	115	4.2	18.0
Catfish	103	3.1	17.6
Chub	145	8.8	15.3
Cod	78	0.3	17.6
Crappie	79	0.8	16.8
Lake Herring (Cisco)	96	2.3	17.7
Lake Trout	168	10.0	18.3
Lingcod	84	0.8	17.9
Muskellunge (Muskie)	109	2.5	20.2
Perch, Yellow (Lake Perch)	91	0.9	19.5
Pike	88	1.1	18.3
Roe (Carp, Cod, Haddock, Herring, Pike & Shad)	130	2.3	24.4
Roe (Salmon, Sturgeon & Turbot)	207	10.4	25.2
Salmon, Chinook (King)	222	15.6	19.1
Salmon, Coho (Silver)	136	5.7	21.5
Smelt	98	2.1	18.6
Sturgeon	94	1.9	18.1
Trout, Brook	101	2.1	19.2
Trout, Rainbow (Steelhead)	195	11.4	21.5
Walleye	93	1.2	19.3
Whitefish	155	8.2	18.9